# Access your online resources

*Learning Through Play for Children with PMLD and Complex Needs* is accompanied by a number of printable online materials, designed to ensure this resource best supports your professional needs.
Activate your online resources:

Go to www.routledge.com/cw/speechmark and click on the cover of this book
Click the 'Sign in or Request Access' button and follow the instructions in order to access the resources

T0386621

# Learning Through Play for Children with PMLD and Complex Needs

This book examines the development of play skills and schemas to support children with learning differences and physical disabilities in learning to play. It highlights the need for appropriate playground equipment in all school settings that educate children with physical disabilities and sensory needs to ensure equal opportunities for outdoor play.

Several play approaches for meeting sensory needs are discussed including Lego therapy, Art therapy, Sand play and Soft play. Digital play for students with physical disabilities is an important chapter in the book. Role play and the ways in which virtual reality and psychodrama support anxieties that some students have is another important chapter. There is also a chapter devoted to parents on how they can support their child at home and how the school can support them.

At the end of the book there is a plethora of resources that readers can copy or adapt to suit their setting. The book provides support for those managing outdoor play for these children at peak times of the day. It shows how play-based learning can work in a classroom setting; the importance of sensory profiles and sensory play; and how play therapy can aid neuroplasticity.

**Ange Anderson,** M.Ed. is a SEND consultant and advisor for schools, specialising in therapeutic and technological interventions for additional learning needs.

# Learning Through Play for Children with PMLD and Complex Needs

## Using Purposeful Play to Support Cognition, Mental Health and Wellbeing

Ange Anderson

Routledge
Taylor & Francis Group

LONDON AND NEW YORK

First published 2022
by Routledge
4 Park Square, Milton Park, Abingdon, Oxon OX14 4RN

and by Routledge
605 Third Avenue, New York, NY 10158

*Routledge is an imprint of the Taylor & Francis Group, an informa business*

© 2022 Ange Anderson

*British Library Cataloguing-in-Publication Data*
A catalogue record for this book is available from the British Library

*Library of Congress Cataloging-in-Publication Data*
Names: Anderson, Ange, author.
Title: Learning through play for children with PMLD and complex needs : using purposeful play to support cognition, mental health and wellbeing / Ange Anderson.
Description: Abingdon, Oxon ; New York, NY : Routledge, 2022. | Includes bibliographical references and index.
Identifiers: LCCN 2021042316 (print) | LCCN 2021042317 (ebook) | ISBN 9781032073590 (hardback) | ISBN 9781032073576 (paperback) | ISBN 9781003206538 (ebook)
Subjects: LCSH: Children with disabilities--Education. | Children with disabilities--Recreation. | Special education--Activity programs. | Play therapy.
Classification: LCC LC4026 .A64 2022 (print) | LCC LC4026 (ebook) | DDC 371.9--dc23
LC record available at https://lccn.loc.gov/2021042316
LC ebook record available at https://lccn.loc.gov/2021042317

ISBN: 978-1-032-07359-0 (hbk)
ISBN: 978-1-032-07357-6 (pbk)
ISBN: 978-1-003-20653-8 (ebk)

DOI: 10.4324/9781003206538

Typeset in Optima
by MPS Limited, Dehradun

Access the Companion Website: www.routledge.com/cw/speechmark

# Dedication

This book is dedicated to the memory of many students that I have had the privilege to teach yet have had short lives because of their illnesses. It is also dedicated to the memory of a wonderful teacher, Heather Lawson who died of pancreatic cancer at a young age. She pioneered the Forest schools approach to learning through play at Ysgol Pen Coch.

# Contents

# Contents

# Figures

# Tables and downloadable resources

# Acknowledgements

I would like to thank all the staff of the special schools that appear in this book. I would particularly like to thank Donna Roberts, head of Ysgol Hafod Lon in Penrhydeudraeth, and Chris Rollings, head of Hadrian school in Newcastle for their photos of outdoor play provision. I would like to thank Julian Lewis, assistant head of Ysgol Pen Coch and Rhona O'Neill, head of Ysgol Tir Morfa in Rhyl for their feedback on how the pandemic has affected play provision in special schools.

Special thanks go to Clare Downey, Hadrian school's Outdoor Education coordinator, for her feedback on the importance of outdoor provision at their school.

I would like to thank Dave Matthias, who runs the cycling programme at Ysgol Tir Morfa in Rhyl who gave up his time to discuss with me how the lives of their students have been changed with the introduction of learning through cycling.

# Abbreviations

| | |
|---|---|
| ABA | Applied Behaviour Analysis |
| ADHD | Attention Deficient Hyperactive Disorder |
| AI | Artificial Intelligence |
| AIST | Association of Integrative Sandplay Therapists |
| ALL | Accreditation of Life and Living |
| ARR | Assessment, Recording and Reporting |
| ASC | Autistic Spectrum Condition |
| ASD | Autism Spectrum Disorder |
| BAAT | British Association of Arts Therapists |
| BSL | British Sign Language |
| CCTV | Closed Circuit Television |
| CLDD | Complex Learning Disabilities and Difficulties |
| CPD | Continuous Professional Development |
| DBS | Disclosure and Barring Service |
| DfE | Department for Education |
| DIR | Developmental, Individual-differences, Relationship-based |
| EBD | Emotional Behavioural Difficulties |
| EHCP | Educational Health Care Plan |
| EPDM | Ethylene Propylene Diene Monomer (synthetic rubber) |
| FMS | Fine Motor Skills |
| HLTA | Higher Level Teaching Assistant |
| HSE | Health and Safety Executive |
| IBP | Individual Behaviour Plan |
| ICT | Information and Communications Technology |
| IDP | Individual Development Plan |
| IEP | Individual Education Plan |
| INCA | International Review of Curriculum and Assessment |
| LA | Local Authority |
| MLD | Moderate Learning Difficulties |

| | |
|---|---|
| MDS | Mid Day Supervisor |
| OPAL | Outdoor Play and Learning |
| PECs | Picture Exchange Communication system |
| PMLD | Profound and Multiple Learning Difficulties |
| PSE | Personal and Social Education |
| PTUK | The UK Society for Play and Creative Arts Therapies |
| RfL | Routes for Learning |
| SaLT | Speech and Language Therapy |
| SEN | Special Educational Needs |
| SEND | Special Educational Needs and Disability |
| SIP | School Improvement Plan |
| SLD | Severe Learning Difficulties |
| SMDS | Senior Mid Day Supervisor |
| TA | Teaching Assistant |
| ToM | Theory of Mind |
| TEACCH | Treatment and Education of Autistic and related Communications Handicapped Children |
| UN | United Nations |
| UNCRC | United Nations Convention for the Rights of the Child |
| UV | Ultra Violet |
| VIP | Venture Into Play |
| VR | Virtual Reality |
| WAG | Welsh Assembly Government |
| ZPD | Zone of Proximal Development |

# Introduction

A special school or unit is made up of talented professionals who continuously develop that professionalism to meet the diverse needs of the students they teach. The way that they teach those students will depend on how those students learn best. We discovered that in a primary-aged special school it is possible through a play-based approach.

It has been the practice for some schools to buy in therapists in the delivery of a play-based therapeutic approach to learning. To my mind, it makes cost-effective sense to offer the study of the therapies as part of teacher training and teaching assistant training for those wishing to work in the field of special education. This puts teachers and teaching assistants, working with students who have special educational needs, in the position of qualifying as therapists in areas that interest them. This was an approach that I led as head of a special school and that the Welsh inspection service Estyn praised us for. This approach enables a school to offer more therapeutic play sessions to more students. I found that the professional development offered to staff made them feel valued and important to the school. Indeed, they were important. In turn, it enabled us to develop a successful play-based approach to learning.

## A play-based approach for adults

I am not sure I remember the importance that play played in my early development and yet without it, I would not have had such a happy childhood. I believe that desire to play, if developed appropriately, stays with us throughout life.

Several summer recesses ago I spent the holidays researching Lego-based therapy as a possible additional play therapy to introduce into the special school that I was head of. I decided against it. I decided that staff members would not be able to stop themselves from helping children with the construction and I reported my decision back to staff.

A year later I was attending church when the minister got out a load of Lego for us all to 'play' with. He felt it would help us plan the future of the church. He used Lego Serious Play® which is based on research that shows that this kind of hands-on, play-based learning produces a deeper, more meaningful understanding of an organisations' possibilities. Playing with actual Lego enthused

DOI: 10.4324/9781003206538-101

me for the task at hand. I felt like a child again. As soon as the church meeting was over, I went straight to a toy shop and bought several boxes of Lego. That is the power of being actually able to play with something rather than just reading about it.

The following day was a training day in school and although the training had been planned months in advance my introduction to the training day had not been finalised. I introduced the training day with Lego Serious Play and Lego-based therapy. Each group departing for their training venue in the school was given a box of Lego with visual instructions. They could complete it as and when they had time but only if they chose to.

It was the most successful training day that we had as a school. It is hard to find a more satisfying payoff than a completed Lego set. The staff even chose to return to their constructions during the lunch break. The camaraderie amongst staff was palpable. At the end of the training day, I apologised to staff for presuming to decide for them twelve months previously. We introduced Lego-based therapy into the school that term. It is the therapy that most schools asked us to provide training for.

As a headteacher, I introduced many conferences and training days at our school. The most successful training days that I delivered, enjoyed by staff, and visiting attendees alike, were those that had an element of play in them. Society for a long time was influenced to expect that when we became an adult, we should put away childish thoughts (1 Corinthians 13v11). Yet feedback from our conference session leaders told us that actually when allowed to play adults were more engaged and enthusiastic. I found that the usual psychological shackles of adult responsibilities that censor thought processes were unleashed when they were able to play. As the Lego introduction to a training day shows it does not require a big school budget for staff to unwind, to be fully present, and to tap into their childhood selves. Play is a hugely important part of everyone's life. It is, simply, fun. We learn best when we are enjoying ourselves. We want to do those fun activities again and again.

Our school ran international conferences on the use of therapies in education. In October 2015 Kevin Spencer, the founder of Hocus Focus™ and widely considered the leading authority on the educational and therapeutic benefits of magic in the classroom, was our key speaker. I had met him in Poland the year before where we both spoke at an education conference, though he was their key speaker. I remembered his talk because he was so much better as a speaker than the rest of us. He had allowed us to play. Even better he taught us magic tricks that we could play on others. He agreed to come over from America to our school to give a spellbinding introduction to our conference where every member of the audience took part in playing and perfecting magic tricks. Our school became research partners with Kevin's organisation Hocus Focus and today the school still delivers magic therapy as a playful learning approach to improve cognition, motor skills, communication and social skills whilst developing play, creativity, and flexible thinking. If you wish to introduce this into your school, please visit http://www.hocusfocuseducation.com

Csikszentmihalyi (1990), an eminent Hungarian psychologist, devoted his life's work to identifying the different elements engaged when the mind is in a state of 'flow'-when a person is completely immersed in an activity with intense focus and creative engagement. Absorption in a task indicates the absence of the self, and a merging of your awareness in the activity you are engaged in. I would go so far as to say the staff found that sense of flow when engrossed in the Lego construction and completing a magic trick.

Our school had been chosen by the Welsh government to develop and pilot a new curriculum for Wales. It was important that I introduce the new curriculum to all staff and governors in such a way as to create a wave of excitement over the new curriculum. At the end of a term, you worry that staff will be tired from a busy term and perhaps forget the new initiatives that need to be put in place. Hence, training days that introduced initiatives were planned to be on the first day of the term which often meant preparation during the recess. I had decided to introduce the training day with a popular children's game. Pass the parcel is a game routinely played by children at parties. At home, the day before I carefully wrapped eight large parcels using different coloured tissue paper for each layer so that no one accidentally unwrapped two layers at the same time. The final layer was wrapped in children's wrapping paper to signify to attendees that they would be playing a childhood game. I put slips of paper with the discussion topics and a gift in each layer between each sellotaped wrap.

On the training day, I played popular music and distributed a parcel to each of the eight tables. Each table sat up to ten people. When the music stopped the person with the parcel in their hands opened the first wrap, kept the gift then read out the aspect of the new curriculum which was discussed for 5–10 minutes at each table before the music started again and participants moved on to find the next aspect of the new curriculum for discussion. Because they were engaging in an activity that attracted them, they focussed their attention exclusively on the task at hand. What is more, since they were doing it for fun and there was no effort involved, they were willing to play at it more. I am convinced that I would not have had the same success if I had stood in front of them lecturing them on the new curriculum. People came up to me throughout the day afterwards saying how much they had enjoyed playing the game, the excitement of opening the gift, and the discussions about the new curriculum. They were enthusiastic, engaged and looking forward to introducing the new curriculum into our school.

The main advantage of play is that young and old alike are putting their abilities into practice almost without realising it. If adults understood the new curriculum better with an element of play included, then it made sense that using play to deliver aspects of the new curriculum would work too. Particularly as the cognitive age of students matched the developmental stages of play.

# A play-based approach for children

Vygotsky believed that children's abilities could be perfected through play. He believed that play is a fundamental tool for cognitive development. Every child has a right, enshrined in the United Nations Convention on the Rights of the Child, to quality play experiences. In the world today many children are denied that right (Sahlberg & Doyle 2019). The opposite is true of special schools where that right to play is enshrined in school policies (see resource chapter for sample policies). I have found in my many years of working in special education, both in mainstream schools and special schools, that a play-based approach to learning works best. Of course, we must recognise that each student in a special school or unit (or a child in the mainstream with an individual education plan) has their own individual needs and these must be recognised in the provision of play opportunities.

# Delivery of a play-based approach

This book will look at the stages of play development and the importance of play schemas for anyone wanting to understand students with learning differences. It will demonstrate the different types of play-based approaches that enhance education. From sensory play and the importance of sensory profiling through the role-play and the undeniable benefits of virtual reality. From the importance of the developments of digital play for those students who are unable to move to how we can support parents with play opportunities outside of school time. From Lego to sand play and play-based DIR classrooms. From creating playgrounds that give equal opportunities of play for students with all kinds of disabilities. To how we manage outdoor play at peak times. This book will demonstrate how you can meet those needs and, as a result, lessen behavioural incidences.

It will give both parents and professionals ideas and resources to encourage a more successful approach to life and learning. A play-based approach.

# The importance of play

We know that there is a cognitive gulf between humans and animals and yet animals, particularly during their early years, naturally involve themselves in play. Some animal researchers say that the types of play they enjoy prepare them for later in life, for hunting, for survival, for burning off energy or strengthening social bonds. There are many entertaining Youtube videos of animals at play. If animals require to play to make sense of their world it stands to reason that humans do too. Play is how animals and humans, especially their young ones, are designed to learn.

As part of an INCA (International Review of Curriculum and Assessment), Bertram and Pascal (2002) reviewed the early years curriculum including the pedagogical and assessment approaches of 20 different countries across the world. Despite differences in the specific curriculum models of those countries, there was a strong consensus on the importance of play in the early years. Many of the students that I have taught in special schools, regardless of their chronological age, have a cognitive age of less than three years of age which suggests that they are at the early years stage of learning. They may remain at that stage all of their lives. Stephen et al. (2003) in their research review for Scotland into meeting the needs of children from birth to age three state that 'a subject or knowledge-based curriculum does not meet the needs of children less than three years of age'. It makes sense to me that all students with a low cognitive age learn best through play.

Scottish MP Beatrice Wishart said in 2021 "By learning together through play children develop the skills needed for trickier tasks and are better prepared to shine in areas of numeracy and literacy". Whitbread et al. (2017) suggested that studies of play with objects in the development of mathematical abilities have shown positive results. I know that in our school we could not have taught maths as well without the use of Boo Zoo and Numicon (both play-based approaches to numeracy – see Appendix 1 for more information). Play must be present *before* any meaningful learning in the classroom can take place (Tait 1972). I have found that teaching through play is a successful way of engaging reluctant learners in education.

DOI: 10.4324/9781003206538-1

# An appropriate education

We need to bear in mind what we wish our students with PMLD and SLD to learn. What is an appropriate education? Here, I shall mention just two of the play therapies – Dough Disco™ and Magic Therapy™ that were used at the school I was head of (there are others further on in the book). They both offered students the opportunity to develop their gross and fine motor skills; increase their self-efficacy, self-esteem, group interaction and interpersonal skills; increase their attention and perception; develop their motor planning skills and develop their cognitive skills. They are both play-based approaches to learning and students enjoyed the activities (see Appendix 1 for more information and the resource chapter for policies you may wish to copy). Both approaches are certainly more appropriate and fun than asking a child who has fine motor skill problems to trace over words or copy write. Particularly when holding any implement may be difficult for them. I have supported students in the past with facilitated learning where I have supported their wrist to enable them to touch an iPad or BigKeys keyboard (go to https://www.Bigkeys.com for more information) if they have intimated that they want the 'write', that is, not the same as putting a piece of paper in front of them and doing hand over hand mark making. By all means have a table set up with paper and markers for students to choose to go to but please do not force them. You will do more harm than good. Think instead of the strength needed to squeeze and roll dough then manipulate it into sausage shapes. The more our students practice through play the stronger and more controlled their arms, hands and fingers become. That is more helpful to them than trying to mimic a mainstream education. A child with fine motor skill issues may have the ability to eye point and this may be the avenue of communication that needs pursuing. I feel that these approaches are what special schools can excel in.

# The right to play

If we look at Article 31 of the United Nations, it states that every child has the right to relax, play and take part in a wide range of cultural and artistic activities. What does the right to play look like for a child with PMLD or with multiple disabilities, sensory processing disorder or visual and auditory impairments?

Through working in special schools, I am constantly reminded that I can never fully appreciate what another human being feels or understands, and every single child should be given the opportunities to play that we all have. Sometimes we need to adapt those opportunities so that they are more easily accessible. The ability to put block on top of block may be affected by the limitations in upper limb movement and control, visual impairment or hearing loss and not cognitive ability. Although it is claimed that all children begin to play weeks after they are born (Parten 1932 – see Appendix 2). I think we may need to intensify scaffolding support and for much longer periods for those born with sensory, physical impairments or sensory processing disorders so that they have equal opportunities to develop play skills. Assistive technology can also help. How do we know when a student with PMLD has had enough of play? In much the same way as we would know a baby has. They may turn their head away, close their eyes, cry or make noises of discontent. It is then time to reduce the stimulation and give them time to recharge. Do not put them off by making it seem like work. Always maintain a playful approach. You will then be in tune with their cognitive level of understanding.

# Developmental delay

Tröster and Bambring (1994) suggested that blindness, especially in the early years of life, leads to severe restrictions on having natural experiences in the world. He added that these restrictions reduce the potential for cognitive and social learning in blind infants and pre-schoolers and could be reflected in developmental delays in play behaviour. I believe this is also true for those born with severe or profound learning difficulties. As it is difficult to assess cognitive ability in someone with multi-sensory impairments then we have to be mindful that sometimes it could be motor difficulties that delay or prevent the acquisition of complex functional play rather than cognitive ability. It stands to reason then that children with special needs will usually have delays in play. Children's early play begins with indiscriminate actions on objects – picking up and dropping, banging and/or mouthing all objects. They move on to taking objects apart and later begin to put them back together again, putting them in and out of containers. Children with special needs have information processing difficulties and so we need to query whether enough time has been given for them to get the desired response to them pushing an object off their wheelchair table – top due to motor problems. What we also have to be mindful of is a person's ability to develop learned helplessness – because a student's late response is ignored or missed. Then being looked after becomes the priority and is an easier option if their attempts at communication have ended in frustration.

If play is an activity for learning, then interventions in play might be useful to help children learn life skills. Delays in play progression may compromise assessment and intervention planning for these children. Vygotsky regarded play as *"an adaptive mechanism promoting cognitive growth"* (Rubin et al. 1983) but to assist some of our students to play we may actually need self-adaptive mechanisms of technology. If children cannot learn by the way we teach, then we need to change the way we teach. If children cannot learn to play through traditional methods, then during this 4th Industrial revolution that we are going through technology could provide the answer and support.

# Assessment of play

There are a variety of frameworks in the UK for assessing students with severe or profound and multiple learning difficulties. These include Routes for Learning (RfL) and Quest for learning as well as the Engagement Model. There are also frameworks which focus on early childhood development such as the early years foundation stage profile and the early years development journal. As they relate to early childhood development these frameworks provide ideas for activities that lend themselves to a playful approach to learning. All of these frameworks can be found easily online. Our school used RfL and B Squared, which is an assessment package that schools can buy into. For more information go to https://www.bsquared.co.uk. All schools should have a planning, assessment and recording system in place so that student's achievements and progress can be reported accurately to parents.

Many play assessment instruments and frameworks are also available around the world (Liffer et al. 2011) and distinctions between their uses and purposes should be considered. They vary in terms of the age range of interest and the levels of specificity for developments in play against which children are evaluated. Play Wales, for instance, has a framework for quality assessment about the delivery of play but I found that it did not cater for children with special needs. Appendix 2 in this book provides examples of different theories on the development of play and these different theories along with the cognitive ages of students should be considered when selecting a play assessment for use. Learning to play is the precursor to learning to learn. We need to understand how a child learns to play.

# How we learn

German educator Friedrich Froebel pioneered the play approach to learning way back in 1837. The term kindergarten was invented by him. Sir Frederick Bartlett (1886–1969) introduced schemata into the world of education and psychology. Goffman (1974) would call them frameworks. To my mind, schemas or frameworks are basically like computer programmes in the brain that can be accessed quickly to understand a specific event or situation. They are a bank of thought processes from our experiences that have been saved and stored for future use to make sense of our world. We all use schemas. If you are visiting a restaurant, you have a schema that you have in your brain for what to expect in a restaurant. You adapt this schema as your experiences of restaurants change so that the schema is up to date.

Piaget's theory of cognitive development (see Appendix 2) provided an important dimension to our understanding of how children develop and learn and grow their schemas. You may have observed some students with special needs constantly repeat an action as if to make sense of the world around them and find out how things work. This can be interpreted as schematic. Schematic actions help the brain develop and aids cognition. Schemas are formed initially in early childhood. As a lot of students with learning differences are at an early cognitive stage they can remain within a particular schema for a very long time until they feel confident. If the schema they have learnt is a negative schema it takes a lot of unlearning. Virtual reality (VR) can support this to great effect.

I have seen students with autism repeat an activity time and time again. I have also seen the results of a student with autism who took apart the school vacuum cleaner in order to make sense of how it worked. It was a pity he could not put it back together and the school caretaker learned to keep the cupboard locked after that. The caretaker also ended up locking the door to the utility room when the same student became fascinated with the school washing machine. When I became headteacher of a brand new school I had learnt to ensure that these rooms had locks or coded door access. All of us never stop learning and adapting our own schemas.

Many of our students require repeated schematic actions to help their brain develop and override any fright/fight/freeze/appease state in the brain. In the same way that we need to understand our students individual sensory profiles, we need to understand which play schemas interest them the most so that we can support them and help them to modify any maladaptive schemas.

Marvin Minsky, the world famous computer scientist, reintroduced the schema and framework construct into psychology in the 1970s as he attempted to give computers artificial intelligence. During the 1970s Chris Athey, principal lecturer in education at the Roehampton Institute, set up the Froebel Early Education research project. Details of the project and its findings can be found in her book (Athey 1990). The book introduced us to schemas of play. Educational writers concerned with play have since come up with the nine most common play schemas (repeatable behaviours) seen during play.

It is very important to encourage the progression of schemas in order to support student's development. In a special school or classroom, we do not teach to the majority, but we cater for individual differences. It is only by observing these individual differences that we can support students. All staff need to be trained in the observation of students play schemas. Observations will inform planning and aid progression.

## Different play schemas we can observe

Trajectory schema is when students like discovering how things move. A child with a trajectory schema may seem to run around a lot and like to climb and jump off things. They may signal that they wish to be pushed high on a swing. They may like to push things off from their work tray (if they have one attached to their wheelchair) to see what happens. They may also like to play with running water and could flood the school toilets if left unattended. If this schema is not understood and supported students could throw larger items, such as a chair, and possibly hurt other students. The schema is all about the fascination with movement. Supporting the need for this schema could involve giving students the opportunity to have a session of basketball first thing in the morning. As well as supporting a student in the development of schema you are also supporting other sensory developments such as proprioception. Special school staff are adept at understanding the needs of students and all staff must be given the confidence, through regular appraisal and CPD to feel able to make these suggestions so that we avoid unwanted behaviours that generally happen because a student has formed a maladaptive schema as a result of the schema not being properly directed.

Transporting schema is when students repeatedly carry things around with them and may repeatedly bring you things. We found with a certain student that we had to empty his pockets when he left Lego club room as he enjoyed hoarding things in his pockets and carrying them back to the classroom to continue the play. A garden area where they can sort and transport fir cones, sticks and leaves might encourage them to develop this schema, and nobody minds losing a few fir cones. In one school that I worked at one of our students supported the caretaker at the end of each afternoon with collecting up toys from the playground and returning them to the right classroom. This helped him to find a purpose for his transporting schema.

- Enclosing schema is when a student constructs fences and barricades for themselves or toys. We have found that some of our students like to make dens or go into a classroom den to relieve their stress. Many of our students with this schema respond well to a TEACCH workstation when they have specific tasks to complete as this is a more enclosed space than a wide open classroom with no boundaries.
- Orientation schema is when students turn themselves and objects upside down, back to front. They may look at the world from different directions. Climbing walls are immensely popular for this and also helps physical development. If you have a policy and risk assessment in place, then climbing walls are a fantastic addition to any school that has students with this schema. It allows them to address a sensory need and they can return to class ready to work. (see resource chapter for policy and risk assessment you may wish to adapt).
- Rotational schema. You may have seen students regularly self -stimulate turning themselves round and round as it is meeting a sensory need. They may want to turn taps on and off. In one of the schools that I worked in we had several students who enjoyed turning taps on and off and the caretaker was kept very busy. If the laundry room has not got a lock on it, you might find a student in there watching and listening to the washing machine go around and around. We invested in a school roundabout so that students could experience going round and round with an adult close by for support. Some students with autism need more sensory information and can spin on a roundabout for ages without feeling queasy like many of us would. This schema can also show itself where a student repeatedly rotates a puzzle piece or uses a fidget toy.
- Enveloping schema is when they are covering, swaddling or hiding and weighted blankets can aid students who feel the need to progress through this schema. It is beneficial if parents are encouraged to buy these blankets as they can aid sleep for some students. Fidgetbum is a patented sleep aid for children with this sensory need and is often recommended by occupational therapists. To find out more go to https://www.fidgetbum.com.
- Connecting schema is when they are wanting to join items together. They would love to play with Lego and other construction toys. It is possibly why Lego therapy is so popular.
- Positioning schema is when they place objects in lines, patterns or rows or stack objects on top of each other. This is something that many parents of children with autism notice first about their child – the positioning schema. This can include wanting their food in a certain order on their plate or sitting in a certain place regularly. It is something that we all have to a certain extent. I can certainly recall as a young teacher not daring to sit in certain chairs in the staffroom. It only becomes frustrating if it begins to take over theirs and your life. A student may lose control if someone interrupts their positioning attempts and so a safe space is needed where their construction can be left until you all agree it is time to put it away.

## Understanding play schemas

Understanding play schemas can help us to provide what our students need for their learning to progress. It is important to share this information with parents. Once parents understand what a schema is and how important schemas are they do tend to stop worrying and are only too willing to support their child. Schema therapy was developed by Dr Jeremy Young. It aims to support people in moving on from a maladaptive schema that impacts negatively on their life. Our brains all work in the same way. Schemas become brain data that our students access when they are told they are going to the dentist for instance. They remember the last occasion and it might not be a nice memory but is their automatic thought. At our school, we developed the use of play therapy, role play and virtual reality to help students move on from these maladaptive schemas, but this takes time and repetition so that they can adapt to the new schema. This is what specialist teaching is all about – teaching students how to cope with life itself. If we cannot teach students how to cope with life itself then there is absolutely no point, in my opinion, in teaching Pythagoras theorem.

## The importance of play

If Piaget, Vygotsky and Parten are right and play forms the basis of all learning then students with severe or profound learning difficulties and a low cognitive age should perhaps have a play-based education. In the next chapter, we look at how special schools have devised their outdoor provision to meet the needs of all students. This is costly but essential to ensure equal opportunities for all. All schools that have children with disabilities must provide the correct playground equipment or else those students will not be able to play. It is time that school inspection teams inspected ALL schools to ensure equal opportunities for outdoor play. I welcome a report on this.

# 2 Outdoor play

'The right to play is the child's first claim on the community. Play is nature's training for life. No community can infringe that right without doing enduring harm to the minds and bodies of its citizens' (David Lloyd George 1926). Outdoor play supports children's physical, cognitive and emotional development.

## Play-based learning

Working with students with complex needs brings its own particular challenges, whether it is in a special school or a unit within a mainstream primary or secondary school. Staff in these settings undergo a lot of training. Teachers in these settings do the same training as teachers in ordinary classes in mainstream schools. Then they have to train to understand complex educational needs, medical needs and manual handling requirements. They have to learn to sign, use communication aids and specific technical skills such as eye gaze to deliver an appropriate curriculum. They have to attend behaviour management training and a host of therapeutic interventions. Continuous professional development (CPD) is the most important spend of any school budget. Staff in these settings need more training days to ensure that staff get the necessary training to meet the needs of the students. If they do not meet these needs, through a lack of training, then I guarantee that behaviour issues will be a major concern.

A curriculum for students with special needs often requires play-based learning due to their cognitive stage of development. Teachers and support staff need to be trained in the cognitive stages of play and play-based learning. Students in a special school require structured play or scaffolded play as students need to learn how to play and to be included. There is a trend at the moment for students to just be allowed to play freely without any support but children with severe or profound special needs cannot play freely without being guided or supported. In some instances they will always need this support. They will need support because of their physical, sensory or communication disabilities or because they just do not understand other children's intentions. In Chapter 4 I show how the DIR floortime approach provided some of our students with the freedom to self-direct play.

DOI: 10.4324/9781003206538-2

In order to deliver play-based learning for students with PMLD or SLD, the playground facilities need to meet their needs. Outdoor play should be available throughout the day to students with special needs. You may decide to timetable its use, but you may also decide that certain areas need to be available at any time throughout the day so that individual students' sensory needs met. Students may not be able to walk or move unaided. They may find the business of an ordinary playground is a sensory overload. Many will have difficulties communicating and interacting with others. In this chapter we look at how special schools have made the most of their outdoor areas to provide play opportunities. You may wish to purchase the equipment described to ensure equal opportunities for all of the students in your setting.

# CCTV and safeguarding

I have found it very beneficial to have CCTV installed in playgrounds. They have been useful in providing evidence if an accident occurs and they protect both staff and students. Students with dyspraxia can easily stumble and fall. Parents/carers of children with special needs often have social service involvement. These parents/carers need to assure the social services that the big bruise on their disabled child's leg can be accounted for. Parents are not being difficult when they demand to know why their child has come home with marks all over their legs. A quick look at CCTV may show you that the child had been learning to ride an ability bike in school that morning.

It is important that playgrounds have gone through safeguarding checks. Students in a special school are particularly vulnerable. Often, they cannot communicate. I remember inspecting two special schools in 2019. When I visited one school it was going through an investigation due to an incident that occurred on the unsupervised playground where no CCTV was installed. The teacher on duty had left the playground to deal with an injured child, and no other member of staff was on the playground to witness the incident. In the other school, the new Head Teacher had changed the entrance to their school and installed CCTV because previous to her appointment, the school playground was used as a shortcut for the public to get to the local shops. It is no good waiting for an incident to happen before you tighten up on safeguarding. If you are part of the senior management team and you have concerns – act on those concerns. If you are an ordinary member of staff and have concerns report them (in writing if you wish to keep a record). Protect students and staff.

I come from a large family. One of my sisters fell off a public playground slide as a child and lost her two front teeth. Another sister fell forward at the front of a five-seater rocking horse and needed stitches in her chin. I went over the handlebars of a bike and still have the scars to remind me. Risk/benefit approach whatever you intend installing so that you are confident it is as safe and beneficial as it can be for your students who have additional needs.

# Outdoor play provision

The foundation age curriculum in all schools allows for outdoor play provision and many primary special schools use the foundation stage as a template for the whole school due to the cognitive age of the students. This means that outdoor play happens throughout the day at primary special schools and the play provision is adapted for older students so that it is age appropriate. This is very different from most mainstream schools who seem to have reduced outdoor play times across the globe (Sahlberg & Doyle 2019; Gray 2013). Although outdoor play provision lends itself to all areas of the curriculum it is particularly suited to the development of PSE.

Outdoor play allows for more self-regulation for our students. It helps them to develop independence as they acquire new skills, cope with the transition from inside to outside play, play cooperatively, follow rules and take turns using outdoor apparatus and vehicles. Outdoor provision allows for the zone of proximal development Vygotsky introduced and scaffolding (see Appendix 2) whilst also encouraging free play. Students with physical difficulties, communication, social and emotional needs often require support so that they are able to enjoy play and develop play skills. It is vital that all support staff are trained to support students to develop play skills as these are the precursor to learning to learn. Due to the cognitive ages of students in a special school outdoor play is as important as it is in any early years provision. Therefore outdoor play provision is a priority. Funding needs to be found to ensure equal opportunity for play is given to all students regardless of their disabilities.

# Planning a playground for students with special needs

There are many things to take into consideration when planning the playground of a school that has students who have special needs. I opened a new special school in 2009. The local authority had planned the build and the interior but had totally forgotten about the outside. Three special schools had closed and students at those schools had been consulted over their preferred name for the new school and were involved in creating a piece of artwork for the new school. They had not been consulted regarding their future playground outside.

When I took up my post nine months before the school opened its doors, I was dismayed to see that the fencing already installed around the perimeter of the school was just 3 ft high and could be easily climbed. On the other side of the fence, there was a pond and a short distance away there was a park. In my experience of working in special schools that was an open invitation to some ambulant students to climb over and head towards the pond or park to play. I had to insist on a 6 ft fence being installed for safeguarding purposes. Luckily, by coincidence, another school in the authority had refused such fencing for their school and we were able to have it.

In the summer term, before we opened in September, I discovered that there was no budget for equipping the playgrounds we had. Knowing how much students in my previous schools had depended on outdoor play I could not contemplate having no outdoor provision for September. I managed to raise some funds and contacted a well-known playground company Playforce.co.uk. They offered to install robust specialist play equipment over the summer holidays in time for us to open. All playground equipment must be installed to meet the European Safety Standard for playground equipment BS1176. Before installing any playground equipment, you need to have a chat with a representative from the local authority and seek their approval for the contractors that you have in mind. You would always keep your governing body informed.

You also need to plan areas or zones throughout your outdoor spaces so that you are meeting the needs and interests of your students. Specific play equipment and apparatus need to be purchased, maybe in stages if you do not have all the funding. Playground apparatus for children with special needs is very costly. Due to students' disabilities, for instance, you will need different types of swings, roundabouts and slides if you are going to ensure equal opportunities for play. Added to that you will need a quiet zone where there is no sensory overload where students can sit and play quietly with appropriate sensory-friendly toys as sometimes a busy playground can create a sensory overload for some students. We had three separate playgrounds in our school separated by the building itself and so once we had been open a couple of years, and finances allowed, we had a quiet zone developed for each playground. These quiet areas were also roofed, and classes sometimes used them as outdoor classrooms during lesson time to develop a theme. I remember one class decorating an outside quiet area to resemble a jungle. It was then left like that for a week for other students to experience during outdoor play.

# Types of swings

*Figure 2.1 Bird's nest swing at Hadrian school*

For as long as I have taught children with autism, I have observed how the swing relaxed them. Swings provide both vestibular and proprioceptive input soothing their overstimulated senses and increasing their balance and coordination. The rocking and swaying sensation seemed to calm them. A set of swings was installed by Playforce in the summer recess before we opened our school. The swings were an immediate success and 10 years on they are still as robust as the first day. They have been used constantly throughout the day, not just at specified play times. If a student with autism was having a difficult time and was a bit overwhelmed, they could be accompanied out to the swings for several minutes of vestibular sensory input. They would regain their ability to concentrate. Safety surfacing also has to be installed under swings, around slides, etc. and must adhere to the current standard for impact-absorbing playground surfaces in the UK (BS EN 1177).

A bird's nest swing was purchased from Playforce that allowed students with PMLD to use a swing. They were hoisted on so that they could be free of their wheelchair to be able to lay back and enjoy the vestibular sensory stimulation. The bird's nest swing proved popular with the rest of our students and as the swings are quite large it meant it could take up to three primary-aged children at a time.

There are other swings that will accommodate wheelchairs. I found, in my many years in special school education, that staff constantly asked for a wheelchair swing but once it was purchased, they rarely used it with the students, due to the time needed to set up and put away. However, Ysgol Pen Coch were recently able to purchase a wheelchair swing from Anbakgard in Denmark for £22000.00. It is quick and easy to set up and has additional seating for peers or staff to join the student. Julian, Ysgol Pen Coch's assistant head tells me that it is a big hit. To see how easy, it is to set up go to https://youtu.be/vh4NSOTULdA. I always said that if someone designed a wheelchair swing that is easy to use, they would make a lot of money. Seems Anbakgard has done just that.

*Figure 2.2 Wheelchair swing*

*Figure 2.3 Close up of securing system on wheelchair swing*

# Playground equipment

A robust climbing frame was also purchased from Playforce as well as outdoor sandpits (with protective covers). Outdoor shades had to be added to protect students in sunny weather. Installing outdoor shades can cause issues. We do not have a huge amount of sunshine in Great Britain, but the sun's rays can damage the skin. We were not allowed to have canopies attached to the new build as the architect assessed that the new build would not carry the weight. I saw this as a design fault that they should have borne in mind before the build was agreed upon. Sail canopies were regarded by the local council as an invite to local teenagers to misuse once school was closed for the evening. We were allowed to have portable canopies that our caretaker kindly put out each day. It is essential to get consent from parents for staff to apply sunscreen and for the school to have a policy. Please see the Resource chapter for a template you may wish to adapt.

We had rubber EPDM wet-pour coloured graphics laid onto parts of the playground by Playforce so that the students could play hopscotch or follow numbers in that zone of the playground. I know that there are many companies that offer this, and they can include pretend roads, roundabouts, etc. for students to ride the bikes and scooters on. Rainbows, flowers, birds, rockets and animals can also adorn the playground floor and its worth chatting to the school council to get the students to vote for their preferences.

Year on year we fundraised and added playground equipment. I managed to find a local company that produces playground equipment suitable for all abilities promoting inclusive play. These were GL Jones Playgrounds Ltd in Bethesda. They have a website https://www.gljones-playgrounds.co.uk. They are an award-winning company that also provides inclusive playground equipment for local parks. They will make bespoke pieces to suit student needs.

They installed a trampoline in the floor of the playground in 2011. The students school council had requested one. We had an indoor trampoline already but because of height restrictions, ambulant students were unable to use it. It made sense to have a trampoline put where there would be no height restrictions. It is a very sturdy outdoor trampoline, and it is wheelchair friendly. It is not as large as we would have liked but it cost us £12,000 then. Photos of the trampoline can be found in my book on therapeutic trampolining (Anderson 2020). When you consider that a wheelchair friendly roundabout cost us £12,000 again in 2013 you begin to realise why it takes a while to get the playground that suits the students' needs and wishes. Fundraising was a never-ending task for me. It is worth bearing in mind that ordinary mainstream schools often have children who have physical disabilities who would benefit from the same playground equipment that allows wheelchair users and children with special needs to play alongside able-bodied children. If you are not catering to these students, then you could be in breach of the equalities act.

Inclusive musical instruments can be added to another zone of the playground so that students who enjoy chimes, drums, pianos or practically anything musical can have the opportunity to play music outside with very robust inclusive musical instruments. You will find that by having zoned areas you get to see what interests your students the most and develops their learning through play.

*Figure 2.4 Musical chimes at Hafod Lon*

GLjones installed an inclusive play unit from their flagship AbilityRange that allowed wheelchair access and ramps that could be climbed using hand holds. They also installed an inclusive roundabout that allowed wheelchair use.

*Figure 2.5 Inclusive roundabout at Pen Coch*

Climbing trees was a popular pastime for children many years ago. Schools today would not be encouraged to plant trees specifically for students to climb. Instead, a purpose-built climbing wall is popular in many schools today. Again GLJones.uk provide sturdy versions that I can recommend. For those of you who are planning a new build and wish to give your students the opportunity to climb higher than a tree, you may wish to copy schools that have installed a 2-storey climbing wall indoors (which will also accommodate wheelchair users). Go to http://www.ysgolgogarth.co.uk to see one in action. A climbing wall, whether inside or out requires intense and focussed mental concentration plus the physical ability for staying on the wall and specific equipment. The able-bodied student will work on their core, upper arms, forearms, shoulders, fingers, hands, abs and calves. It will build muscle strength, endurance, agility and flexibility. If you have the space to create a climbing wall then I advise you to visit http://www.rockclimbingcentral.com which has videos of wheelchair users accessing climbing walls, the benefits that they get and lots of other useful information to help you make an informed decision. Climbing walls require a policy and risk assessment. These are included in the resource chapter for you to adapt for your organisation if you wish.

# Sensory play garden

At Ysgol Pen Coch we had a sensory play garden installed when we opened so that our students could explore the world through using their senses. The garden was made up of herbal plants and flowers that gave off a smell as the students passed the plants or touched them. The garden was wheelchair friendly. The plants that students liked the best, often picked or reached out for, were lavender, curry plant, thyme and honeysuckle. Some of the plants had a texture that students liked such as Lamb's ears, heathers, grasses and salvia. Bamboo was also popular. We snaked a path through the sensory garden and the garden led to the students entrance and exit to school. This allowed our students the opportunity to repeat the sensory experiences at least twice daily. Many of our students continue to work at the sensorimotor stage of development and need sensory re-inforcements to strengthen brain connections and aid brain development. Often students would choose to meander through the garden and play amongst the sensory smells, the windchimes and the water fountain. I believe that when they choose to meander through the sensory garden, they are telling us that they need this reinforcement in order to make sense of their world. It is more difficult for students with PMLD. Often in wheelchairs, with no communication, reliant on an aide to walk them through the garden. How can they let us know that they would like to spend more time in the sensory garden? It is vitally important to develop the use of eye gaze and other tech-nologies that will allow our students to communicate their needs and wants.

The garden had several wooden archways along the walkway. Windsocks and windchimes hung from some of these. Students would be confronted with the reflection of themselves as they reached midway and encountered the outdoor full-length mirror. On one of the archways, we hung strings of plastic balls (that you find in ball pools) so that children saw bright colours and felt the light touch as they passed through. We replaced the wooden archways twice in 10 years (due to rot) and I would suggest that a robust tubular steel archway might prove longer lasting such as the ones from http://www.agriframes.co.uk that come with a 10-year guarantee. In the middle of the sensory garden, we had an interactive sculpture that the students made with a local artist, and this also doubled up as a bird feeder.

As well as the sensory garden we had a few quiet garden areas in the school, and these contained seating areas with sensory planting and even mini beast hotels. They were away from the playground areas and tended to be used during lesson times. These were areas for quiet reflection and are much needed in a special school where some children get sensory overload from busy classrooms and need to chill. To sit outside in nature and to be still is sometimes all that is needed for students to retune their minds and their senses.

# Hafod Lon Penrhyndeudraeth

Not all authorities forget playgrounds in their planning for new special schools. Donna Roberts, head of Hafod Lon, opened a new school in 2016 in Penrhyndeudraeth. The architects there met with the students and asked the students to draw or give them photographs of what they would like. Donna then asked staff in the foundation phase what was important to them. Donna and her staff believe that the development of play skills should be given great prominence. She believes children learn through play. The staff and students asked for a covered area, a messy play area, slide and swing, a place to run and a separate place to use bikes and scooters (for safety reasons). Donna had a bike store built. I wish our authority had been as thoughtful. If you are involved in a new build, then I would suggest that you insist on the playground being a priority as it took me years to fund and develop a good enough playground whereas Donna had an excellent playground all ready for the students when her school opened its doors.

*Figure 2.6 Bike store at Hafod Lon*

## Bikes

The Key Stage 2 and 3 curriculum at Donna's school builds on skills learnt in the Foundation Phase taking account of the additional learning needs of their students. Aspects from the

Foundation Phase Framework are used when appropriate to enable all learners to access relevant skills, knowledge and understanding at an appropriate level as directed by the Welsh Assembly government. Key Stage 2 staff at Donna's school asked for a climbing frame, slide, swings and a roundabout. They too wanted a covered play area and plenty of space to run and a bike store. Please see the Resource chapter for a lesson plan involving the use of bikes. In the photo that Donna kindly shared you can see two different types of adapted bikes. We followed the Bikeability level 1 course at our school. Bikeability is a government-recognised training. For more information go to www.https//:bikeability.org.uk

A third type of bike that we used at our school was the Ezyroller ride on bike, which is a cross between a go-kart and a bike. It sits low on the ground and can be hands free, the legs and feet push against the foot bar. It became so popular with all ages in school that although we started off with 6, we ended up with 18 of them. They fold up easily and are easy to store. These are not bikes to learn to ride out in public on but they were recommended to us for students with dyspraxia as they encourage coordination and dexterity. The Ezyroller has received numerous awards. To find out more go to http://www.Ezyroller.com

The staff in the secondary department of Donna's school asked for a climbing frame, football and basketball pitches and a trim trail. This ensured that the students could still play at any time during the day in an age-appropriate setting. Students in the secondary department who needed to use the wheelchair roundabout or swing would access it during their play time sessions, which were at a different time to Key Stage 2.

## Ysgol Tir Morfa Rhyl

Dave Matthias works at Tir Morfa. He found that the Post 16 students behaviour improved when they were given the opportunity to play and work with bikes. He was so impressed by the difference that bikes seemed to make him and his assistants qualified in cycle mechanics and Cycle Wales sponsored their external verifications. This enabled them to service the bikes regularly and ensure that students could use them daily.

In 2018, Post 16 students were invited to do City and Guild qualifications in bike mechanics. They repaired old bikes and used the money to buy special needs bikes, including wheelchair bikes to ensure that every student had the opportunity to ride a bike for pleasure if they wished. So far 22 students at the school have achieved entry level and 4 students have achieved level 1 City and guilds. The Wheels for All campaign aims to make cycling accessible for all ages and abilities and is supported by the Steve Morgan Foundation. They provide a setting at Marsh Tracks near Rhyl for the students of Tir Morfa to use. During the Covid lockdown, Tir Morfa set up its own cycle track, complete with zebra crossing, in its own car park so that students could continue to enjoy cycling.

Older learners at Tir Morfa with PMLD have the opportunity to take part in Accredited National Award Schemes that support their learning aims and afford recognition for their achievements. The Accreditation of Life and Living (ALL) Award Scheme and the Duke of Edinburgh's award scheme can both be used to great success and develops their leisure and play opportunities outdoor.

# Hadrian School Newcastle

Hadrian School is a special school in Newcastle upon Tyne for students aged between two and eleven. Chris Rollings is head of the school and felt that outdoor play was so important that he appointed an outdoor learning coordinator. The school staff pride themselves on having a creative and engaging curriculum. They have a whole school Outdoor Learning Topic Calendar that incorporates all areas of the curriculum and provides children with a broad and balanced learning experience. Their school policy is to teach outside a minimum of 20% of the school week. However, during the Covid pandemic learning outdoors became more important than ever for the school. Government advice on being safer outdoors mid pandemic resulted in their agreed outdoor teaching time to become part of their daily routine. This was one of the conditions for students who were on-site during the COVID 19 pandemic to keep them safe.

Learning at Hadrian school is cross-curricular, and linked to the students' individual outcomes, many with a focus on developing engagement. Outdoor play lends itself to practical engagement and appropriate risk taking.

Clare Downey, the school's coordinator for outdoor learning said "Children need these opportunities in order to build their confidence, spatial awareness and physical strength. Having new and inviting resources and areas outdoors can allow teaching and learning to come alive".

All of the class teachers at the school are extremely proactive and plan for the use of outdoor areas in all weathers. They have a wealth of outdoor resources such as a Mud Kitchen, a Water Wall, a Yurt, an Adventure Playground, a Caterpillar Garden with a fire pit and a large wooden train. They have a Secret Garden, an Early Years Playground, an Internal Quad, a Trim Trail, an Outdoor Art Classroom and a decking area. They even have their own Stagecoach Bus that is fully working and allows for role-play and practicing road safety skills and travel in the community.

Each student at Hadrian School has a bespoke EHCP that drives their learning and ensures that they receive the appropriately balanced curriculum matched to their needs. All of the areas of their EHCP can be met in various outdoor learning play spaces.

In particular, the Mud Kitchen is timetabled to each class for one session per week and is extremely popular with all of the students. The Mud Kitchen allows students to learn new skills that will benefit their life in the long term, such as self-confidence, sharing and turn taking, problem solving, creativity and role play, early math and literacy skills. The Mud Kitchen has a water supply, mud, leaves, pots, pans and cooking utensils. Students access the Mud Kitchen in various ways depending on their needs, such as, creating and following recipes, exploring colours and textures, discovering how ingredients affect properties, role-playing their home life, developing their fine motor skills and increasing their tolerance of wet and messy textures. They explore using their hands and feet, to squish and squelch, feeling different sensations and showing responses and preferences to a range of sensory experiences.

Figure 2.7 Mud kitchen at Hadrian school

Clare informed me that they recently had a Yurt built on the grounds which is fitted with a log burner so classes can re create real life experiences of holidays and camping. The Yurt is timetabled for a day to each class on a rolling rota so that classes can theme this space for a day. Classes have made soups, hot chocolates and curries or decorated them to become a sensory experience e.g., Halloween, light and dark, etc. Classes use the Yurt for storytelling and music sessions. With a log burner inside it always feels warm and cosy regardless of the weather. It is a great place to observe the weather, even snowfall.

Figure 2.8 Inside the yurt at Hadrian school

Hadrian special school relentlessly looks to provide new experiences and add to their repertoire of resources. Their latest project aims to rejuvenate the Caterpillar Garden and decking area. They have wood tree trunk seating with spaces for wheelchair users around their fire pit. There is a large wooden train to create role-play for a real-life experience of travelling on a train. Many of their children do not have the opportunity to go on holiday and travel, and one of Clare's aims is to create memories and experiences they can treasure.

Clare told me of an example of how outdoor learning has impacted the learning of one of the children at Hadrian school. She said, "Daniel is a nine-year-old boy who has complex additional needs. Dan has daily seizures which require constant adult supervision and monitoring. He is a delightful boy who accesses a physical and therapeutic curriculum. His engagement levels through his school day are documented to allow adults to see what motivates Daniel to allow a bespoke and personalised timetable. This is essential as Daniel is an early stage communicator: he makes choices and shows preferences physically through gestures, facial expressions or choosing objects.

As Daniel's sensory engagement profile began to form, it was documented that he showed much more engagement when he was outdoors. This information was used to direct his timetable to become more outdoor focussed. The impact this had was tangible.

Recently, Daniel has begun using a more formal means of communication. He now uses a core vocabulary board to make choices (This board with symbols on is made up of the most used vocabulary for a child, known as their core vocabulary). Children begin with a 2-word choice board, and for outdoor play using the words 'stop' and 'more'.

To make a choice, children touch the symbol and adults respond appropriately. This process is modelled initially by adults to encourage a link between the word, symbol and action. Daniel has jumped from using the 2 symbol board to a 6 symbol board. He used 'stop' and 'more' so efficiently that he is now working on 'fast', 'slow', 'help' and 'go'. Outdoor learning has given Dan the opportunity to find a voice and open up a whole new world of possibilities for him".

If you wish to find out more about how Hadrian school uses its outdoor play areas for learning and to see photos of these then please visit https://hadrian.newcastle.sch.uk/curriculum/the-school-curriculum/outdoor-learning/

# Forest School play area

The idea of Forest School originated in Scandinavia and was introduced into the UK in 1993. From around 2000 Wales began to support Forest School with local colleges beginning to train for Forest School programme leaders.

*Figure 2.9 Entrance to Forest School at Hafod Lon*

Forest School areas are the ideal environment for experiential learning, offering physical opportunities of running, jumping and climbing as well as a treat for the senses such as experiencing the weather, sounds, smells and textures. Students can get involved in problem solving with real-life play experiences such as how to build a den using natural materials. Some schools are lucky enough to have a woodland environment on site that can be used whilst other schools use local woodlands that lend themselves to Forest School education. Forestry Commission Wales has been a supportive partner to schools in Wales. The teacher/student relationship is fundamentally different from traditional teaching as the child leads the way in learning to play and to experience space, movement and sensory stimulation encouraging and stimulating curiosity.

Heather, one of the Forest School leaders at our school, provided me with a Forest School report for the autumn term.

"During this term, the children were introduced to the safety rules of the Forest School and the safe use of tools, and they became familiar with the environment through exploration. Children began to use an increasing range of tools appropriately for their purpose and carried out activities accordingly. During the term, children cleared weeds from paths prepared the raised beds ready for planting in the spring and explored the wooded area making sure it was a safe environment for them to access. Children carried out various activities – mini beast hunts, collecting various leaves and twigs for collages, identified various leaves and trees, made leaf crowns, leaf printing, identified birds, bird watch, made bird feeders using different materials, collected blackberries to make fruit fools and explored the wood area using their senses to listen, see, feel".

Classroom-based activities included woodland management, posters to identify bird species, creating artwork, logging the afternoon's activities, playing games and workbooks. Children are encouraged to work independently and as part of a group. Please see the Resource chapter for a copy of the long-term plans for Forest School.

Heather wrote "These are the benefits that I have observed as a Forest School leader:

> Forest School encourages curiosity, exploration skills, use of all the senses, empowers children to use the environment, increases co-operation with their peers, supports spatial awareness and motor development. It promotes Self-regulation, risk challenge and adventure. It gives students the opportunity for self-determination, social competence, problem solving and unstructured play. I found that it helped creativity and imagination developed. It moderates child obesity and enhances inventiveness and self-reliance. It reduced anxiety and depression and developed resilience and agility".

As Head Teacher, I devised a risk assessment and a Forest Schools policy. Both of these can be found in the Resources chapter for you to adapt to suit your school or facility. An outdoor play risk assessment and an outdoor play policy can also be found in the resources chapter.

The OPAL (Outdoor Play and Learning) Community Interest Company helps make play better in hundreds of primary schools and early years settings and has pilots in Canada, Australia and New Zealand. They have developed a set of best practice principles that will help create a nurturing and inclusive play environment that can be seen here: http://outdoorplayandlearning.org.uk/

## Effects of the COVID-19 pandemic on outdoor play

The lack of play opportunities during the period of the Covid pandemic certainly concerned child psychologists and education experts. Members of www.Playfirstuk urged the government to relax the restrictions and asked the government to prioritise social and emotional wellbeing once the lockdown was over.

In February 2021, number 10 Downing St confirmed that although children could use community playgrounds, parents who take their children to a playground to exercise could not socialise and had to stay two metres from anyone not in their household. In Wales and Ireland, it was very similar. Play England tweeted in February 2021 "We as paediatricians would like to see a national agenda for play, let's use it to start the healing". In Scotland, children were luckier. They were given the right to outdoor play allowing up to thirteen under-11s to be accompanied by two adults outside (Play Scotland 2020).

During the period of the Covid pandemic, schools were told to reduce unstructured play to ensure social distancing. Students in most schools could only use the school playground in their classroom bubble. This meant that at least they did get to play with others from their class during school time. Outside of school, it was a very different matter.

I am in contact with many special schools in England and Wales, and they all remained open during the pandemic through some alternated classes so that children had a week in school and a week of home learning (supported online by staff). Only half of the classes were in school at any one time which made the playgrounds more accessible. Other special schools remained open only for looked after children, children on the child protection register and those whose parents were key workers. The remaining children accessed online learning provided by the schools. This meant that a lot of students were not having any outdoor play unless they lived in Scotland.

The impact of lockdown on child and adolescent mental health cannot be ignored. Social isolation has exacerbated the conditions that many of our students with special needs are vulnerable to. Parents of children with special needs on the whole cannot afford the specialist play facilities that a purpose-built school has. I believe these children have suffered the most during the Covid lockdown. Ordinary children have found the restrictions hard to understand. Children with special needs may never get over it.

# Digital play outdoors

Active outdoor play seems to have been declining before the pandemic possibly due to parental fears of stranger danger, risks of accidents and inclement weather. These fears need to be addressed if we are to get children back into the habit of playing outdoors. Long gone are the days when the only parental rule was to be home by dark. The freedom to play unsupervised that earlier generations were allowed are in the past. Technology means that we are reminded constantly of the dangers. Yet let us turn that on its head and use technology to provide safer play outdoors. Today drones can accompany children outside where parents can keep a check on them and the weather. It is true that in this technological age outside play can include Pokémon Go and the Interactive Play Network Map. Both of these have been seen to encourage students with special needs to get outside and exercise (Robinson 2016).

Digital play does not have to be a sedentary occupation. Pokémon Go is a prime example of how a digital augmented reality game can improve health and wellbeing as well as develop many other skills. It is nonsense to suggest that digital games do not encourage exercise. A joke that did the rounds on social media was that it took Michelle Obama eight years to convince people to go outside and be active and Nintendo (through the use of Pokémon Go) did it in 24 hours.

Think of the Wii fitness games available. They not only improve health, but the game-playing strategies also develop problem-solving skills. I have seen first-hand how social skills developed between two students with autism using a Wii game. To see these two students support each other in a Wii game go to https://youtube.com/watch?v=j_k3S8Ed1ds&feature=share. There are new high-tech digital outdoor playgrounds available. Visit http://www.playgroundcentre.com to find out more about their smart playgrounds. The play has just moved on from skipping over a rope that is all. When would you rather be playing? Now or then?

In the next chapter, we will look at how a playground is managed at peak times such as during the lunchtime play period.

# Lunchtime play for students with special needs

When my daughter attended primary school and returned home at the end of the day, she was always asked what she had done in school that day. The only times that were important enough for her to remember were the playtimes, particularly lunchtime play. If you have a child that attends school, you might try asking them. Think back to your lunchtimes. No, not the ones in secondary school when you went down to the chip shop. The ones in primary school. What did you do? What kind of playground facilities did you have? Would they have been good enough for children with learning differences or physical disabilities?

## Staffing

In a primary special school, outdoor play provision is used throughout the day. In this chapter, we will concentrate on the lunchtime playtimes as these seem to warrant extra policies, rules, risk assessments as well as extra staff. The reason for extra staff should be obvious. All school staff need a lunch break themselves. There are regulations regarding this. This means that staff must take it in turns to have a half-hour for lunch during an hour lunch break for students. In many special schools and pupil referral units, teachers agree to do a lunchtime duty so that the students and mid-day supervisors (MDS) have an experienced member of staff to go to immediately who understands all students' physical, cognitive and emotional difficulties. Teachers overall have a half-hour lunch break, like teaching assistants, plus a half-hour preparation time for the afternoon lessons. You can check these regulations out along with the number of directed hours teachers are expected to work at www.gov.uk. Headteachers who employ teaching assistants employ them on contracts that specify their hours. This contract usually specifies a half-hour break for lunch. There are regulations as to how many hours an assistant can work without a break. You can check this out through a union such as Unison and I would always recommend that whatever role you take on in a school that you join a union.

Students with autism who engage with peers on a playground often show significant physiological stress (Corbett et al. 2010). There is a need to teach coping strategies in addition to fundamental social skills to our students with special needs so that they can cope during playground

DOI: 10.4324/9781003206538-3

breaks. You cannot put these responsibilities on a mid-day supervisor. My experience has taught me that students with special needs still need a teacher or higher-level teaching assistant (HLTA) to oversee lunchtime play to support the development of these skills. When we play with others, we learn about turn-taking, sharing, other people's feelings, waiting, giving and taking. Students with special needs require scaffolding to acquire these skills. Play is not actually written as a curriculum subject in schools, but it probably should be. Although lunchtime supervisors are employed to support students during this time, they do not have the experience of the different learning needs and physical disabilities and so cannot be expected to always have the answers. Please see the resource chapter for mid-day supervisors (MDS) job description that support students with learning differences that you may wish to copy or adapt for your workplace. I have found, as a special school headteacher, that MDS feel supported when they have other teaching assistants who know the children and a lead person to go to if there is a problem.

## Scaffolded play

Lunchtime play is an escape from the usual structured environment of the classroom and gives students the freedom of choice that some seem to need. When they direct the outcome, when they explore, when they do things that are important to themselves. On a playground full of students with special needs this must be done through a supportive scaffolded approach. It is also the time when children get to have the chance to recharge their batteries as it were. If you work in a school, you will feel a difference in the school atmosphere when the weather dictates a 'wet lunchtime'. There is evidence that unstructured breaks from cognitive tasks improve learning and attention (Whitbread et al. 2017). It is important that students are given a break, but research shows that it is not important whether the break is sedentary or vigorous and that levels of attention increase as a result of just having a break from the classroom (Pellegrini & Bjorklund 1997). In my experience though, from many years of 'wet lunchtimes', I would say that the majority of students like to get outdoors.

The hallmark characteristic of autism is impaired reciprocal interaction (Corbett et al. 2010) and students with PMLD are rarely, in my experience, singled out as playmates. Although we may encourage our students to play with others, I have found that this often needs to start off as a guided or scaffolded play.

## Inclusion or segregation?

We regularly sent a group of students across to the mainstream school that we were cojoined to for lunch and lunchtime play. Often parents are keen for this to happen. If parents do not wish it to happen then it does not. When we asked the students what they liked about going across those who could communicate told us it was the cafeteria styled lunch and using different playground facilities. Hardly any of them enjoyed playing with mainstream students and some of our students opted to return to our playground after eating lunch. We regularly sent senior staff over to observe and the feedback was that our students did not know how to initiate play with the mainstream students.

Sending students across to the mainstream school meant we had to employ extra staff to accompany them. The staff that we were able to send tried to encourage interaction, but it was rarely successful as the mainstream students also did not know how to interact with our students. No teacher was on duty in the mainstream school. Decisions and supervision were left to the mainstream MDS.

When we first started sending our students over it appeared that some of the mainstream students were taking an interest in our students. The then deputy head informed us at a campus meeting that she was bribing her students with house points. On another occasion we discovered a couple of mainstream students bullying our students. They lost house points and their parents were informed by the mainstream headteacher. It is important to constantly monitor and evaluate inclusive play-times with the same rigour that we monitor and evaluate the curriculum. It is important that parents are given this report. It is important to discuss inclusion with parents on a termly basis and certainly if an issue arises. I remember a parent coming to see me to inform me that her child was not sleeping on a Tuesday night and did not wish to come to school on a Wednesday. The child could not speak but was letting us know that she did not enjoy lunchtime inclusion. It only happened for her on a Wednesday. When we stopped lunchtime inclusion the sleepless nights stopped.

# Behaviour

Behaviour is a big issue for school staff during free play. Gavin Williamson, the minister for education in 2021 wrote that maintaining good behaviour was essential, especially after the Covid lockdown and that 'Out of control behaviour will destroy the wholesome and happy environment that every school should have, leading to bullying, and turning playgrounds from a place of joy to a jungle'.

I may have been fortunate, but I have never seen any bullying in any of the special school playgrounds that I have supervised or observed, as a teacher, a senior manager or as an inspector. Any behavioural issues that I have seen on a special school playground have been because of communication difficulties. Students in a special school can misinterpret social cues and have difficulty resolving conflicts independently. Behaviours can exacerbate during lunchtimes when students must learn to play alongside other children than their classmates. When they must share objects, take turns, develop social skills, and make friendships. These skills are hard enough for ordinary children to master by themselves but for children with special needs play must be guided.

Vivian Gussin Paley says in her book *The Boy Who Would be a Helicopter* that the golden rule of childhood was that one must not do to a child what you would not want done to yourself. "As my teaching errors have not been punishable by isolation, humiliation and denial of activity, I would not impose those sentences upon the children" (1991).

# Zone of proximal development

The lunchtime playground could be regarded as the zone of proximal development for learning social skills (see Appendix 2 for Vygotsky's ZPD) and its importance in a special school setting cannot be taken lightly. That is not to say that absolutely all play needs to be scaffolded or guided. Indeed, a study by Smith and Dutton (1979) suggested problems that were more challenging and required creative and innovative approaches by allowing the children to play freely got better results. Psychologically, it is all about creating a playground of opportunities for play so that the students feel free to play with what they wish to play with yet feel secure and supported to do so.

To alleviate this problem special schools often have zones with space for quiet reflection as well as space for climbing apparatus, swings, slides, trampolines, roundabouts and riding adapted bikes. These will include rota systems for turn-taking that are overseen by adults. Special schools are particularly good at adapting playgrounds to meet the diverse needs of their students. Some schools have communication boards in their playgrounds that help students. A new playground sign at Kellison Elementary in Fenton, St Louis in America was devised specifically for a student with autism and made headline news in 2020. It is like a communication aid that has been enlarged and then plasticized to protect it in all weathers and used widget symbols. Post Mount Communication board for parks, playgrounds and schools can be contacted at shop@ talktometechnologies.com to make a board to suit your school. Many students in special schools have their own portable symbol supportive communication cards. Sometimes they forget them so a large playground communications board can act as a backup and new or temporary staff can easily see the display board. If you wish to find more ideas for developing your own, then a search on Pinterest will give you a selection to choose from.

# Guided play

In a paper written by Tröster and Bambring (1994), they cited eight specific differences in the play behaviour of children who are blind from that of children who are sighted. I would concur on every point and also say that in my experience these are true for students with PMLD and SLD too. They need to be supported in their play, as they exhibit far less spontaneous play than ordinary children, though they do not necessarily need to be directed. Lunchtimes are an ideal time to do this.

Some children find it difficult to cope during this less structured time, and it seems to be compounded by not having their regular class staff with them. Lunchtime staff, who almost all come in mid-day, are not with children at any other times. These MDS sometimes find the lunch hour a challenging time, with children not always responding in ways which they do for known class staff. What do we need to do to help?

Some lunchtime rules are important. These can be written and illustrated using a symbol supported publishing programme so that they act as a visual reminder for students. Students from the School Council should be involved, if possible, in devising these rules. These rules can have a prominent place in the classroom, school hall or corridor and students should be regularly reminded of them. It is also useful to have the lunchtime staff rules on display so that all staff and those students who can read are aware of them. Rules that I have used in the past have included:

# Student rules

Please follow the school Rules "Show me 5" (taken from the Incredible years behaviour programme http://www.incredibleyears.com)

Remember to use kind words

Remember to use kind actions

Please be polite and respectful to lunchtime staff and use a small voice

School Council – please be helpful to lunchtime staff

# Lunchtime staff rules

Staff are to attend regular inset training sessions related to the needs of the students.

Staff to familiarise themselves, with policies, procedures, and risk assessments.

Please ensure that you all take a consistent calm approach.

Please follow the positive behaviour management policy adopted by the school. You will get more of the behaviour you focus on the most. Focus on positive behaviours.

Please familiarise yourself with school rules. They will be symbol supported and displayed on walls for all to observe and follow.

Please help the children to play sensibly outside. You may need to get actively involved. This will reduce behavioural issues.

Please model to students using kind words and kind actions.

Please make sure that you monitor who is going in and out of the building and ensure that students ask permission to re-enter the building so that you are aware for fire safety purpose.

Please ensure students on second sitting have been toileted and washed their hands after play and before entering the hall for lunch.

Please talk with the students calmly, do not shout or respond emotionally to poor behaviour.

Please reward the students for being extra helpful, kind, polite.

If there is a first aid issue, please deal with this appropriately and record the necessary information appropriately.

If there is an issue with behaviour, please report this to the HLTA responsible for behaviour.

Please ensure that students are out of the hall by 1:10 pm and the floor is free of debris so that the hall may be used by teaching staff and therapists.

Follow the lunch play rota for activities such as:

Bikes
Scooters
Swings
Roundabout
Slide
Climbing frame/wall
Indoor clubs
Outdoor trampoline

# Class-based staff rules

- Please ensure morning lessons are ended in time for toileting and hand washing that MDS will assist you with if you are in the first sitting.
- Please make sure that you get back to class in time to receive your class at the end of lunchtime.
- If you are on lunch duty, please make sure that you deal with behaviour matters; lunchtime staff need a point of reference when there are difficulties.
- First aid matters will be dealt with by designated first aiders (who are paid extra for that responsibility).
- Ensure that students know the lunchtime play rota of activities each day.

# Senior management rules

- Ensure risk assessments are in place for every item of play equipment in use
- Ensure risk assessments are in place for any behavioural concerns
- Ensure risk assessments are in place for weather concerns
- Ensure that all staff know what the procedures are for outdoor and indoor play at lunchtimes and have signed that they have read all of the necessary documents
- Ensure that any issues raised by staff are dealt with so that there is a consistent approach

# Play policy

Lunchtime schedules are revised continually at the start of a school year. I well remember, as an assistant headteacher, writing version 26 of the lunchtime schedule during the first month of the school year. To help parents understand and appreciate the benefits of lunchtime playschools should write a Lunchtime Play Policy. This is not mandatory, like for example, a Behaviour Policy. However, it is a great way of avoiding parental complaints about minor injuries. Government guidance from the HSE says that minor injuries do not need to be documented or reported unless they are very serious. Obviously, these minor injuries need to be addressed by qualified first aiders. It is up to the individual school to ensure that this is done and to make the decision on whether to inform parents. At our school, all injuries witnessed were documented and reported to parents. Please see the Resource chapter for a play policy you may wish to adapt for use in your school or facility.

In the next chapter, we shall go inside the school to look at how play can dictate our learning in the classroom itself.

# DIR FLOORTIME™ in a school setting

I have to admit here and now that I am not a fan of Applied Behaviour Analysis (ABA). It is a system used in some schools based on receiving an award for exhibiting a desirable behaviour. Think Pavlov's dogs. In my humble estimation, it does not teach a child to communicate in a meaningful way but to communicate in order to receive a reward. When we opened our school in 2009 an ABA centre locally was closing, and we took on one of the students. We were warned that he was a particularly difficult student with severe behaviour problems. What we found was that in actual fact ABA had just not worked for him. He was a delightful boy and thrived with a different approach. A play-based approach. Since all children love to play, it makes sense to design the curriculum around children's play. It allows students to play to their strengths.

We needed to do something different for students who could not learn in the same way as other students. These particular students could be disruptive in a formal classroom situation. A traditional classroom environment did not suit them, the structure did not suit them. Although our school used a play-based approach to learning it was on adult terms. We used numeracy and literacy approaches based on a play but directed by staff. Students went off to receive in-dependent play therapy, Lego therapy, VR role-play, and we provided in total 24 different therapies that students could access outside of the classroom and decided upon by parents and staff. These students wanted more than that. They wanted to direct the day. Freedom to play and learn for themselves was what seemed to suit them. If we can get the environment right for students, then we give those students the best opportunity to learn. 'The teacher's role is to identify children's learning orientations and using this knowledge to manipulate the learning environment and stimulate their motivation to engage with the environment' (Bruner 2009).

## A child-centred approach

Article 12 of the convention of the Rights of the Child (United Nations 1989) highlighted the importance of children's opportunities to influence decision-making in which their voices should be heard in matters that affect them. Traditional classrooms, with a teacher-directed approach, tends to foster dependence, competition and impedes collaborative decision making whereas a

DOI: 10.4324/9781003206538-4

*Figure 4.1 Play-based learning*

child centred, constructivist approach, which is what DIR lends itself to, encourages engagement, enquiry and adaptability. This might sound like a difficult task in a school that is made up of students diagnosed with severe or profound learning difficulties. We tend to assume that means a low cognitive age yet sometimes it is their physical and sensory difficulties that mask their cognitive ability. Sometimes all they need is the opportunity to direct their own learning through play.

DIR floortime® was originally developed by Dr Stanley Greenspan for parents to use with their children diagnosed with autism. It is now used in some schools too. It encourages the natural interests of the child and what they like to do. "D" describes the personal development of each individual. "I" describes how the individual responds to the world around them. "R" represents the importance of relationships to individual development. "Floortime" is a play-based approach that allows the child to take the lead whilst challenging the child to develop socially, emotionally and intellectually.

John Dewey, a leader of the progressive movement in education in the United States, once wrote about play as "A name given to those activities which are not consciously performed for the sake of anything beyond themselves; activities which are enjoyable in their own execution without reference to the ulterior purpose" (Dewey 1915a). Dewey argued that play fostered experiential learning and voluntary participation. I believe that a well set up DIR classroom exploits the process of play to develop the learning Dewey refers to. However, it is not a cop-out for schoolteachers and assistants. School staff still have to plan but it is a more subtle kind of planning and observation, where the child does not feel he or she is working or that there is an ulterior purpose to their play. There is still a value to assessing performance in a DIR class so that we can measure progress. Montessori regarded play as *"the child's work"* (1967). When you watch a child in a DIR classroom you will see that they are self-directed and appear to be working at a chosen self-initiated task in a completely relaxed state of mind.

# Sensory overload

It is absolutely no use creating individual behaviour plans (IBPs) when it is the environment that is causing the behaviour. We understand nowadays that certain sensory overloads for individuals can result in a negative response. It seems obvious. If you, for instance, hear a baby crying continuously in a supermarket as you try to shop, you could be forgiven for (a) wishing they would leave (b) losing concentration on what you intended buying (c) having a headache or (d) complaining. If you were a child, you might not have acquired the social skills needed to try to ignore the intrusion on your mind and a behavioural response may have seemed more apt. When we are stressed, we do not perform at our optimum. Sometimes busy classes create sensory overload.

We have come a long way in our understanding of sensory overloads. Ear defenders are common practice in many schools today. It makes sense, therefore, that every student entering a special school has an assessment and not just an assessment of their academic ability. That is too easy. In a special school we need to assess each student to create a sensory profile for every student. These are not easy to complete, require time to ensure the profile reflects the needs of the student and is regularly monitored for changes and updates. Dr Greenspan, who developed the DIR floortime approach, in his book *The Child with Special Needs (1998)* suggested that we have to remember that the child with special needs is the best viewed in terms of individual differences regardless of their diagnosis. He recommended that an individual profile is created, and it is that profile that determines the intervention plan not the syndrome.

# A sensory profile

We found that first we need to identify and record:

  sensory-related behaviours and when they occur
  attention issues related to impaired sensory input
  challenges with focus or emotional regulation as a result of sensory needs
  meltdowns that impair functioning and where they happen
  antecedents

Next we need to ask why.

  Is it an unmet sensory need that causes the behaviour?
  Is, for instance, the reason the student chews on their clothes because they need more proprioceptive input?

Then we need to try out some strategies to see if they are effective.

- A record should be kept of activities/strategies used (at home too if possible)
- Working strategies should be added to the students sensory profile (this is a working document constantly updated)
- Strategies that do not work are dismissed, and new ones trialled

Finally, we need to monitor the effectiveness both in school and at home.

A sensory profile template is included in the resource chapter for you to copy and/or adapt. An individual education plan (IEP) may target one or some of the sensory-related behaviours. A template IEP is in the resource chapter for you to copy and/or adapt.

A sensory profile assists anyone working with that student to understand their behaviour and modify their instructions to suit. Behaviours, on the whole, tell us that something is not working for that student. Now you can battle on with trying to get the student to comply with the way that you teach, and you could mistakenly see it as a battle of wills. But you would be wasting important time that you cannot get back and you could be inadvertently sending that student into a meltdown. We are in the 21st century and it is the time that we taught students in the way that they learn and not expect them to learn through the way we have always taught. We need to change, not them.

DIR is a philosophy for intervention that allows you to apply the model in any setting. It is important that all staff using the model are trained in its use. In our school, some teachers, an HLTA and some TAs were trained in delivering DIR in a school approach.

There is currently an online DIR floortime course available. It is a 6-hour course, and more information can be found at – https://www.icdl.com/courses/320

## Stages of play

We noticed the social stages of play (see Appendix 2) more easily once we introduced a DIR floortime class. We noticed the solitary play that one child preferred. He did not seem to notice the other children but would seek out an adult to set up the water tray, which was his preferred mode of play.

Another student would watch others play as an onlooker for a few sessions before attempting parallel play next to them. Two of the students would watch each other construct designs, ask about them before eventually offering parts to the construction and joining in.

Some evidence suggests that children participating in a more formal teacher-directed classroom showed more inattention and stress behaviours, less confidence in their own abilities, less enjoyment and less progress in motor, language and social skills when compared with peers in playful-learning classrooms (Weisberg et al. 2013). Our observations bore that out. In fact, due to the success of the DIR classroom, some of our teachers adapted the approach to their own classrooms.

## Setting up a DIR classroom

In child-centred education the child is seen as 'ultimately the agent of his own education' (Entwistle 1970). This is what we found the DIR floortime approach allowed.

The setting up of a DIR classroom requires a different approach to the more formal classroom.

You may decide not to have an actual TEACCH workstation (find out more at http://www.teacch.com) at all in a DIR classroom to begin with as all adults will constantly be observing children's play for the IEP and IBP targets already determined and shared.

Students often prefer dough disco, magic therapy, using finger paints, construction blocks and threading if they have fine motor skill issues and may be attracted to using an iPad to communicate with rather than a pen or pencil. In a play-based classroom, it is important to let the child lead you in this as you will get more success if you follow their lead.

We found that the students guided us in the development of different play areas within the classroom. Sometimes a particular construction would take up a large part of the classroom for days as students engaged in associative play and cooperative play (see Appendix 2 for Parten's stages of play). The outside area was used a lot by two boys in particular. One of those areas was a wild garden and one student had a particular fascination for bugs. The other student loved to explore through the use of water play and so that was an area that became a permanent water play area for the whole of his time in the DIR class base. This led to a play-generated curriculum, where teachers organised learning experiences around themes and interests that students demonstrated in their play.

We provided a kind of 'maker movement' (see Appendix 1) area where we stored loose parts such as shells, beads, corks, bottle tops, buttons, bangles, pinecones, lids, tubes, containers, trays, guttering, cable wheels, boxes and tubes. Students used them to make whatever they wanted. They became creative and used their critical thinking skills, teamwork, problem solving and negotiation skills. There was no right or wrong way to use them so no fail.

The adult role in the class was similar to that in Lego therapy, as an observer, mediator and facilitator, supporting their ideas but not doing it for them. Please see the DIR report in the Resource chapter on the success of this method of teaching.

Executive functioning skills (learning to learn) is something that many of our students find difficult and so one of the aims of the DIR room was to help our students focus on learning to play. We wanted to help students develop more complex levels of play through their involvement in different play stations as opposed to workstations.

A DIR floortime policy is included in the resource chapter for you to copy or adapt to suit your organisation.

# A typical school day for our version of DIR floortime

## *Registration/choice/scaffolding/observations*

As the students came into the classroom, they were encouraged to put away their belongings. Students may be coached on doing this to start with until they can master the routine for themselves independently. Once their things are organised onto their pegs, they went to the class play area/s. To be honest, we found that students were so keen to go to these areas that they learnt to sort out their belongings fairly quickly.

## Morning circle time/self-esteem/self-expression

Greetings, peer-awareness and interaction. The principles of DIR were incorporated into every aspect of morning circle.

Students were seated in a semi-circle around the teacher. All interactions made by the students during circle were treated as purposeful and intentional. Students were encouraged to engage in extended circles of interaction, whilst staff were mindful of their sensory profiles so that they tailored their participation to students' strengths. The staff never interrupted interactions but might have added to them to make them more complex. This challenged students to make more responses. The students were encouraged to greet their peers and various activities were used to increase peer awareness. Songs and games were usually used as we found that students enjoyed them and remembered them more easily. They were alternated with the more instructional portions of the circle to keep the students focussed. Circle time focussed on group discussions and targeting specific social issues.

## Play skills/peer play/regulation games

This was the time for individual sessions allowing staff to interact with the child at their level, while teaching through meaningful interactions.

These included the ability to sustain attention, engage and develop adaptive and coping strategies. Staff encouraged independent ideas and the ability to sequence these ideas in meaningful ways, but they did not encourage imitation at the start and the start always came from the student and not the adult. The adult might make suggestions once the student has initiated the play but only as a reinforcement and only if the student has consciously expressed a desire for that involvement to further what the student was already trying to do. They encouraged students to problem solve, think and play symbolically and understand emotions and use creativity and imagination. Individual, education plans, social and behavioural goals were layered upon these foundations.

Dewey writes that in the early years for an ordinary child we need to 'get hold of the child's natural impulses and instincts and utilise them so that the child is carried onto a higher plane of perception and judgement and equipped with more efficient habits: so that he has an enlarged and deepened consciousness and increased control of powers of action. Wherever this result is not reached, play results in mere amusement and not in educative growth' (Dewey 1915). I believe this is what our staff were encouraging our students to do through the DIR format. They were allowing the students a constructivist way of learning, giving them a motive for using the materials in real ways instead of doing classwork that had no meaning for them.

Children who perceive an activity as play are more focussed, attentive, motivated and show signs of higher well-being while on-task (Howard & McInnes 2013). Observation notes were taken, and all skills were monitored closely by the classroom staff present during the sessions.

## Semi-structured play skills

Specific play and social skills were taught as part of our therapeutic curriculum. This is a time when students' sensory processing needs were met individually or in a small group setting (allowing for turn-taking and peer interactions to be developed). They included VIP (Venture into Play), therapeutic Lego, play therapy, magic therapy and in fact we delivered 24 different therapeutic interventions. There are chapters in this book describing the way we used some of those approaches in our school.

The staff took on the role of the child and played at their developmental level modelling specific skills. Activities were based on the children's natural motivations and incorporated familiar themes. For example, during play therapy, students may have used dolls to act out riding home on the school bus if that was something that was of concern. Once students became more independent in their play, staff facilitated more sustained peer play.

## Social skills group

Peer awareness and interaction, abstract thinking (building bridges, sequencing, predicting), problem solving, emotions, theory-of-mind, specific social and language skills, attention and independence were all targeted during this time. These skills followed a hierarchy based on the individual needs of the children. Each skill was extensively covered using books, videos, role-play, puppet shows and experience-based activities. After being targeted through a structured lesson, students were encouraged to generalise the skills outside of the circle. Facilitation of these skills followed by verbal reinforcement assisted this process. This took place during class time or during another therapeutic session deemed appropriate. Note: If a child was not able to benefit from this group session, they could choose to receive one-to-one with a therapist and re-introduced to the group when ready.

## Abstract thinking/sequencing/problem solving

Our main goal was to help the students become independent thinkers. Sometimes our students engaged in inappropriate behaviours, lacked social and language skills or seemed self-absorbed due to a poor understanding of the world around them. These deficits were targeted through critical thinking activities. Activities used to target these skills included sequencing events using visuals and toys, role-play, social stories and games. All activities reflected themes familiar to the students. Abstract thinking, sequencing and problem solving were targeted throughout the day incidentally.

## Emotions/art/creativity

This area of instruction was a priority. Teaching the students to recognise and respond to emotions in self and others through experience-based learning promoted independent generalisation of skills. Emotion lessons included discussion, books, videos, puppet shows, role-play and games. Different sensory modalities were incorporated into every activity and self-expression was encouraged during this time.

In addition, students based in the DIR classroom still followed the usual school routines, transitional music cues and protocols. If they chose, as students did, to return to an ordinary classroom within the school at a later date, they could easily transition back into the routine of one of these classes.

## Progress

DIR floortime is still used at the school. Pivotal educational moments were observed in the DIR classroom as students made connections and showed progression and creativity that they had not shown in the ordinary classroom situation. A report by the behaviour coordinator is included in the resource chapter. Students showed a greater than anticipated ability to cooperate with others, improved language skills, decreased challenging behaviour, improved self-regulatory behaviours and acceptance of other student's suggestions when involved in a group project. The experience of play enhanced the students social-emotional, physical and creative skills, whilst allowing them to reach their IEP targets in an integrated manner.

## DIR at home

Parents reading this book can copy the approach used in this chapter but there is also an excellent website http://www.playproject.org that supports parents wishing to use the DIR approach at home.

In this chapter, I have shown how we introduced a completely play-based approach to learning into a class. All students with special educational needs should have a sensory profile as this chapter suggests. In the next chapter, we shall review the importance of sensory profiles and look at how sensory play supports students with learning differences.

# Sensory play

Some special schools and units have rooms dedicated to sensory play. Sensory play is anything that stimulates and encourages the student to build on any skills they may have in an under-developed sensory area or to support a sensory impairment. Students who get their sensory needs met are able to learn more easily.

All of us are sensory beings. Dunn's model of sensory processing proposes four basic patterns (Dunn 2007). You might be particularly sensory sensitive and selective about tastes, food, clothing textures and environmental light and heating. I have a five-year-old grandson who is sensory sensitive. He is extremely sensitive to environmental changes and people's moods. He will chew the cuffs of a sleeve. On the other hand, you could be a sensory avoider and have a low threshold and use active self-regulation to reduce any sensory input. I have a little grand-daughter who is a sensory avoider. She prefers her own room to play with the other two siblings and is a stickler for following the rules. She likes predictability and knowing what is happening next. If you have a high threshold and look for high-energy activities because these activities give you the sensory intensity you need you might be called a sensation seeker. My third grandchild, aged three, is definitely a sensation seeker. She loves spicy food, is always on the go, is full of energy and loves having a brother and sister to torment and get a response from. If you have passive self-regulation, you are not bothered by noise or distractions and might be regarded as easy going but would need some extra encouragement to take part in things. Then you might be known as a bystander. I do not have a fourth grandchild to fit that particular pattern.

It is only if our reactions were extreme in any one of these four areas and that they would interfere with daily life would they need intervention strategies. That is why we do sensory profiling for students in special schools. Most students attending a special school need inter-vention strategies for their sensory issues.

## Sensory profiles

It is obvious to me that we have more than the five senses first proposed by Aristotle but there are disagreements as to how many. Eco-psychologist Michael J Cohen (2007) claims that we have at

DOI: 10.4324/9781003206538-5

least 54 senses at our disposal. He reminds us that the discomforting senses like pain, distress and fear help us to avoid seriously burning our hands on a hot stove. When you consider his list of senses (shown in Appendix 3 of this book) you begin to appreciate why sensory impairments and sensory processing disorders handicap our students in so many ways. It also helps us to understand why the sensorimotor stage of development is the bedrock of a child's development. According to Piaget (see Appendix 2), it is when a child learns through their senses and motor interactions with the physical world. However, many students with learning difficulties and motor problems have sensory processing issues too. This makes it difficult for them to progress easily through this stage of development and though they may move on to enjoy constructional play they may still need to work on the sensorimotor stage of development. It is worth remembering that just as abled-bodied children learn to walk at different stages that this is also true for other developmental milestones.

Some of our students are born with sensory impairment. That is not the same as sensory processing. If a student is blind, partially sighted or wears glasses that is a sensory impairment. If a student has hearing problems and wears a hearing aid, then they have a sensory impairment. Students with a sensory impairment may also have a sensory processing issue but they may not. A sensory profile is needed for every student to determine what kind of sensory therapies and play opportunities are required and whether it is to support a sensory impairment or a sensory processing issue. Sensory profiles are a vital aid to planning, assessing, recording and reporting.

If a student has a sensory impairment, then the sensory support services for the local authority will more than likely have been working with that student's family long before the student began school. The sensory support service has professionals qualified in assessing and delivering support that visit schools on a regular basis and are able to advise schools and offer their expertise.

It can sometimes be difficult to know what a child with complex needs, who may have limited language and low cognition, is able to hear. Once an assessment is made it is important to know what the sensory services advise and what the parents have agreed. Hearing aids? Makaton? British Sign Language (BSL)? All of these will impact the school. I remember employing a Welsh speaking BSL assistant for a specific student who was deaf and from a Welsh speaking household. I remember another student who was deaf but whose parents felt that his autism and his sensory processing were more of a priority. They wanted him to use Makaton and also the picture exchange system (PECs). I recall another student with profound and multiple learning difficulties (PMLD) who was also deaf and whose parents wanted him to have a very music-based curriculum as he seemed to respond to music at home. I have written about how deaf people respond to music in my book Music, Sound and Vibration (Anderson 2021). A sensory profile has to take on board the parent's views and any advice from the sensory services, then a decision on where the sensory support will take place and what resources are required needs to be taken.

When students enter a school, they will have assessments. One of the most important assessments is the sensory profile. A sensory profile will help staff to develop strategies and resources to help the student make progress in spite of their sensory issues. If a student has issues with noise for instance, then you may assign that child some ear defenders, but you would not give ear defenders to every student. If the student requires a sensory diet, then this too would be included on the profile. If you have this information to hand and a new teaching assistant plans a sensory taste game a number of issues can be avoided. The resource chapter includes a template for a sensory profile that you may adapt to suit your organisation.

The therapeutic approach of sensory integration was originally developed by occupational therapist Jean Ayres who was ahead of her time. It is often referred to know as ASI (Ayres Sensory Integration 1989). Sensory integration is known for its play approach to remediation where the activities aim to influence learning and behaviour. It has been used as an evidence-based practice for use with children with autism. A training programme began in 2016 and it is now possible to gain a certificate in Ayres Sensory Integration. Go to http://www.ci-asi.org to find out more.

Many of the students that I have taught have demonstrated either hyper-reactivity or hypo-reactivity. This can impact on their response to others during play and needs to be borne in mind when deciding on an activity. Of course, these should be included on a student's sensory profile. Examples of hyperactivity observed by me and other staff members were:

Distress with certain sounds, e.g., can tolerate loud music but not coughing by another person making associate play and cooperative play difficult.

Discomfort with certain textures making dressing up and role-play a possible issue.

Irrational fear of heights and movement, e.g., cannot go on school roundabout, go on the school climbing wall.

Examples of hypo-reactivity observed:

Disregard of sudden or loud sounds, e.g., some students do not react to the playground bell signals.

Unaware of painful bumps, bruises, cuts, etc. A child who does not mention that they have cut themselves or fallen over during playtime and shows no reaction could lead to school staff being unaware of the issue until a parent informs them.

# Dark rooms

A dark room is a sensory room that once the door is closed is completely dark. This gives students the opportunity to build on any visual skills that they may have through a visual stimulation programme. These programmes are often developed by the local authority's sensory services department for specific students. A dark room provides a stimulating environment to heighten visual awareness in a student's surroundings and allows the observer to find out what other factors may have an impact on how they see.

The sensory vision support team who visited our school would bring equipment with them, such as light-up balls that they would play 'catch' with students. Light-up cubes, stars and other shapes are also available, and these cannot only aid sensory stimulation but teach important maths concepts at the same time. They can help students with exploring their schema play by stacking, rolling, sorting, moving and hiding these objects. As with most learning done in our school, a playful approach tends to get the best response.

On the whole, the visual sensory equipment that I have witnessed being used with students have been objects of play and are fun. Optic fibre sprays, bubble tubes, sensory ball lights, fluorescent toys and materials (good under the UV lighting) are all popular. Glow in the dark mats encourages students to have time out of a chair, lie on the mat and track the lights. There are many multi-sensory light kits now that promote visual tracking and scanning whilst promoting play. Some schools build up a bank of equipment for use in the dark room and some classes keep their own bank of equipment. These are taken to the dark room for use by their own students when they are timetabled to use the room.

The dark room can also be used by the auditory support team as the darkened room prevents disturbances that might disrupt concentration. The room does not need to be darkened though and they may decide to instruct you to alternate with lights on and off during assessment and working with students.

# Light rooms

Another sensory room is often called a light room. This again is a room that could be used by someone from the sensory support team or a member of school staff working on a one-to-one or small group basis to develop an aspect on the students sensory profile. These sensory rooms can help a student to get rid of frustrations they may have encountered before entering the school building. Sometimes a student would go straight to a sensory light room from the school minibus, with a member of the breakfast club staff (all breakfast club staff at our school worked as teaching assistants in our school too) and before classes began. Sometimes we knew an incident on the bus had caused the issue and sometimes it was something that happened at home but often we did not know the cause of their sensory overload. A session in the sensory room could help that student to have a more productive day at school. A sensory session can provide stress relief and proprioceptor feedback. This room was timetabled for use with touch therapy such as TacPac, story massage and reflexology. Classes near to the room would also use it at the start of each day with specific students with sensory overload. Sensory light rooms contain sensory equipment to stimulate the senses and relaxation music. Please visit Appendix 1 for more information on Story massage and TacPac.

# Classrooms

Some teachers choose to have a sensory corner in their own classroom. They may have a dark den in that corner too. Dark dens are available for students to access as a means of relaxation and calming. A box of light/sensory toys, tactile cushions and music should be available for students to play with in the den. Nowadays, there are so many products available, and they are constantly added to. A variety of weighted resources are available to use with children, e.g., vests, blankets, scarves, wrist bands and back packs. These may be used to help a child to calm, to regain focus or to realise where their body is in space.

Teachers also sometimes keep Fidget bags with sensory toys and objects for students to use if needed. Fidget toys provide a focus point that may help students filter out excess sensory in-formation. Some of the sensory toys that would help a student with an auditory processing disorder, or hearing impairment might be resonance cushions, echo platforms, echo balls, sensory percussion toys or ear defenders.

These items and dens can be found on sites that cater specifically for special needs such as https://www.tts-group.co.uk or can even be found on Amazon. Parents can also purchase these items to extend the sensory play at home. If parents are unsure of what to purchase both the sensory support service and school staff are only too happy to advise.

# Sensory circuits

Some special schools use their hall for sensory circuits and sensory-based activities. Sensory swings help students understand the importance of vestibular, proprioceptive and tactile integration as it relates to postural development, balance and physical development. When I was a deputy head at a special school in Herefordshire in the late 1990s, we were lucky enough to have some amazing occupational therapists who were enthusiasts for this kind of sensory play, and they would bring the swing and other pieces of equipment to the school for the day and set it up in the hall then easily dismantle at the end of the day. The hall was timetabled for this and students who benefitted from this kind of play had that opportunity with qualified professionals who would report back to the school and parents. I have not met any other occupational therapists with as much enthusiasm though I feel sure they do exist.

In my last school, where I was headteacher, our teacher coordinator for ASD provision set up our sensory circuit in the hall. This had three areas – alerting, organising and calming and these three areas met specific physical exercises which helped to refine and focus student concentration. The decision as to whether a student should attend circuits was based on advice and guidance from occupational therapists regarding their perceived need to work on the vestibular and proprioceptive senses – motor planning and gross motor skills, balance and coordination.

Sometimes teachers will set up an area in a classroom where there may have room for a small rebound trampoline. I have written a book on therapeutic trampolining (Anderson 2020) that gives ideas on how to use a rebounder to aid sensory processing.

# Soft play room

A soft play room with crash pads will give some students the full-body tactile stimulation they desire. Some students feel the need to bang their heads, crash into walls needing that sensory input. A soft play room allows them to do this whilst keeping safe. At one of the schools, I taught in our Soft play room was two stories high and had punch bags and ropes that allowed students to let off steam. The room contained heavy balls that students could throw knowing they would not hurt anyone but knowing that they could get rid of that surplus energy and use their trajectory schema. No one wants to see a student with pent up sensory issues feeling the need to throw a classroom chair because the school has provided no alternative to meet their sensory needs. Once students sensory needs are met, they are able to focus more and be in the right frame of mind to learn.

*Figure 5.1 Soft play room*

Whatever you decide to do my advice would be to timetable the use of the area or room and ensure all members of staff have a copy of the timetable. A large sand timer can help a student to understand how long they have on the rebounder before returning to the activity they took time out from. There should also be a school policy on the use of these rooms or spaces so that all members of staff understand their use. Staff training is the most important school budget spend. You cannot expect your students to thrive if the staff do not know how to meet their needs.

# Outside spaces for sensory play

Outside play areas can also be utilised to provide sensory input. I know that certain students of ours extensively used the swings to provide a feeling of calm and a vestibular input. Some outside sensory play activities that our students have enjoyed including:

1. Walking – This is a very regulating activity as it provides rhythmical and predictable sensory inputs. Walking up hills and/or wearing a backpack with bottles of water in will increase the resistance which will provide stronger regulating proprioceptive inputs.
2. Den building – Use blankets, throws, tarps, etc. to build as these create a regulating environment and reduce the amount of sensory input the student has to process.

3. Obstacle courses – These provide great regulating sensory experiences. Encourage your child to carry objects to make the obstacle course. Try to include things that will allow students to crawl and have different body positions.
4. Gardening activities – Digging and pushing a wheelbarrow supports vestibular and proprioceptive systems. Visual, tactile, olfactory and auditory senses are stimulated by plants and insects as well as fresh air.
5. Cycling – Supports the vestibular system by promoting the ability to maintain balance and an upright posture. Develops the proprioceptive system and body awareness. Stimulates auditory, tactile, olfactory and visual senses if outside.

## Sensory sensitivities

As I wrote at the start of the chapter, we are all sensory beings but many of the students we teach are particularly sensory sensitive and it is important that we:

Recognise and seek to maximise every student's potential through recognising their sensory sensitivities and differences.

Raise awareness and develop confidence in the knowledge of student's sensory sensitivities and differences through the use of every students sensory profile.

Ensure that the sensory sensitivities and differences of students are supported by the school's wider environment.

Ensure students are provided with the most useful and suitable sensory provisions and remain at the forefront of sensory impairment and integration developments in order to seek to maximise each pupil's potential.

Acknowledge the need to work collaboratively with professionals, students and their families related to their sensory impairments, sensitivities and differences.

For many of our students with sensory processing issues, a therapeutic play approach can support their learning needs. In the next chapter, we shall look at the therapeutic play and how it supports neuroplasticity.

# 6 Play therapy

## Venture into play

Play therapy was introduced at Ysgol Pen Coch in 2009 when we opened. The play therapy that we introduced then was Venture into Play. It had been used previously in one of the special schools that had closed, and staff wanted to continue its use. Venture into Play is a programme available to use from The VIP Play Skills Profile (interactive-connections.co.uk). If you visit that website you can also order the skills profile and find out about training opportunities. If you cannot afford to pay to train a member of staff as a play therapist, then VIP is the next best thing. It is still used very successfully at the school that I was headteacher of for many years. We also sent two members of staff to be trained by PTUK as play therapists, but we continued to deliver VIP by other staff members as it is such a good programme. Please follow the link to see a session in action. Venture into Play Therapy on Vimeo.

The VIP skills profile helps you to identify the student's current play skills with reference to two specific dimensions – the social dimension and the developmental dimension. The profile enables you to record:

- the student's interactions with adults and other students in playful situations
- the developmental stages of the student's play
- identify the progress over time of the student's play skills through dated descriptive comments and the use of a graduated frequency marker
- review the student's profile of play skills, consider the emerging skills, strengths, and weaknesses, and identify targets (for instance we need to be mindful that students who have poor motor planning may find it easier to tip up a basket of toys than have to search through a full basket).

The VIP skills profile does not aim to describe every step in the development of play for individual students, instead, it provides useful markers and signposts.

The profile tackles the social dimension of play that Vygotsky might recommend, the cognitive development of play that Piaget wrote about and Parten's stages of social play theory (all to be found in Appendix 2 of this book).

DOI: 10.4324/9781003206538-6

# Neuroplasticity

Using play as therapy can prove very beneficial to students with autism and ADHD who are often in a state of sympathetic arousal or even the dorsal vagal parasympathetic state (life-threatening) of arousal. When our students are in this state, they have an increased heart rate and their ability to concentrate on anything you try to teach them has gone out of the window as they focus on their perceived threat to life. It sounds dramatic. Try and imagine a gunman entering the class and what you would do as the teacher. I think that you would concentrate completely on the threat to life. The survival instinct takes over. As dramatic as that sounds that is how some of our students live their lives. During the Covid pandemic, many people began to find out how it feels to have a body full of stress hormones.

If you watched the 2020 ITV programme 'I'm a Celebrity' you will have seen a BBC radio 1 presenter, Jordan North, take himself, in his mind, to his happy place to take his mind off the fact that he had snakes climbing all over him, whilst buried in a box. Thinking of his happy place made him feel safe. I know that some of my students had certain toys that helped them cope with their fears. It is our responsibility to help them develop a better response mechanism and this may include the use of these toys and discovering happy places.

It may also be that a play therapist encourages the student to develop new positive schemas to replace negative schemas that were causing that stress. A play therapist will encourage the development of new neural pathways so that the student can cope better in a flight, fright, freeze or appease the situation. This process is known as neuroplasticity. It takes time and a lot of repetition. Teaching students with learning differences is anything but boring.

# Safeguarding

It is important to give students respect when they are having individual therapies. No one should interrupt the therapy or bring a visitor into the session without prior agreement with a therapist and parent/child. I was informed recently of a student whose session was interrupted because the outgoing headteacher thought it was appropriate for the new headteacher to see that the student benefitted from the therapy. Parent, therapist and child complained. And rightly so. Generally, the specific details of the session are confidential. This promotes trust for the student and the safety of the therapy space. A safeguarding issue is the only time that this would change. Information on general themes and progress would be shared at reviews and reports but a student/parent would be told about this beforehand and their agreement sought. We were fortunate to have CCTV in some of our therapy rooms, but a risk assessment should always be done beforehand, and the child protection policy followed.

# Therapeutic play

In 2013, a member of staff began training for a Post Graduate Certificate in play therapy with PTUK. On completion of this course, the member of staff became registered as a Certified

*Figure 6.1 Art therapy*

Practitioner in therapeutic play skills. She was then on the Professional Standards Authority's register of Play and Creative Arts Therapists managed by PTUK. The member of staff completed her training but two years later moved to Australia. Another member of staff volunteered to undergo the PTUK training too and carried on the delivery of play therapy in the school. All the therapeutic play sessions at Pen Coch were overseen by a clinical supervisor and the supervisor was approved by PTUK. Once the member of the school staff qualified, they no longer required this supervision.

Play therapy provided our students with the opportunity to use their most natural form of expression, that of play, to communicate. Play therapy allowed the play therapist to communicate understanding, acceptance, and options in a way that children could most readily take in. Therapeutic play in our school was used for:

- emotional and anxiety problems
- communication difficulties including students on the Autistic Spectrum
- delayed schematic play development
- repetition of skills that have meaning, relevance and importance
- helping students choose positive thoughts

social integration

enhancing parent/carer child interaction

ongoing assessment.

Students are rarely presented with real freedom to play without some form of rules and regulations; therapeutic play allows the student to have the freedom of choice within safe boundaries. As the students are set free from taking care of themselves safety becomes the province of the therapist as the student is neither praised nor blamed. The student is therefore never judged as being right or wrong and provided with a free atmosphere within safe boundaries to express themselves verbally, physically or with playthings. The therapeutic play practitioner has been trained in and follows the guidance from Axline's Principles of non-directive play therapy during the sessions with students.

The therapist will:

forge a relationship with the student that is friendly

allow the student to come to therapeutic play as the student is feeling or presenting on that day

give the student a feeling of being allowed, for them to express completely their own feelings

be aware of the student's feelings and how they show them; to reflect these feelings back in a way that the student gains an insight into their own reactive behaviours

use creative pursuits such as art therapy to encourage the brain to adapt and change and improve brain plasticity

give the student the responsibility to make choices and make changes through deep respect in the student's own ability to solve their problems by providing the opportunity for them to do so

follow the lead from the student without attempting to direct the student's actions or conversations in any form.

not rush the therapy, it will go at its own pace, and it is important for the therapist to recognise this.

not create too many limitations on the session, only those that are necessary for safeguarding and child protection.

The therapeutic play practitioner encouraged our students to use play to share their life experiences, express their concerns and worries and find solutions to problems. The environment created in the playroom allowed the student to feel safe, accepted and understood. This process empowered the student and through play he/she feels a sense of control and mastery. When students are given the experience of a sense of control over themselves and their behaviour it can then lead to feelings of self-worth. This in turn allows them more flexibility in the world and in time they begin to learn schemas that are more enjoyable for the people around them.

At Ysgol Pen Coch we created a playroom that provided an environment conducive for child-centred play.

## Tool kits

These were purchased to meet the recommendations of the PTUK, including:

| | |
|---|---|
| stones, rocks, shells, crystals, marbles | boundaries |
| vegetation | buildings |
| primitive animals | people |
| birds | fantasy figures |
| wild animals | spiritual figures |
| Domestic animals | machines |
| stones, rocks, shells, crystals, marbles | vehicles |
| paper | conflict figures |
| paint | musical instruments |
| containers, glitter, sequins | puppets |
| clay | dolls house |
| glue | mirror |
| books | buildings blocks |
| dressing up | games |
| baby dolls | sand |

## Referrals

Students were referred for therapeutic play either during annual reviews of their statements or from the class teacher. Once a referral had been made the therapeutic play practitioner gathered information on the whole child through clinical forms. Strength and difficulty questionnaires were completed by the class teacher, parents and when appropriate, with the student. Parents were interviewed and given the opportunity to discuss therapeutic targets. Educational targets were also set by the class teacher using the school's assessment programme. The therapeutic play practitioner recorded how the sessions went if targets were met and the class teacher reviewed any impact on the student once returning to class. Termly reports were written, and a review of the student's progress was discussed with the class teacher. An impact report can be found in the resource chapter of this book. Every therapeutic play session was supervised by a certified play therapist during clinical supervision which was scheduled for every 6th session. If a decision was made to end the therapy students were given a planned ending which was built into the sessions.

# Sandplay

Art therapy and sand therapy were both offered as a part of play therapy at our school, but all schools are different. Our first play therapist used sand therapy a lot as her preferred method. Here is a video of this https://www.bing.com/videos/search?q=ysgol+pen+coch+youtube+play +therapy&docid=608002025839201789&mid=1C916C23B10B813A02DB1C916C23

If you wish to concentrate on sandplay here are some contacts: BISS – British and Irish Sandplay Society; a Jungian approach to sandplay. http://www.sandplay.org.uk. http:// www.sandplayuk.uk provides training from the foundation to advanced diploma in sandplay therapy. AIST is the association of integrative sandplay therapists. The association provides details of available courses on its website http://www.sandplaytherapy.co.uk. Please bear in mind the safety aspect when using sand. I recall a parent coming to see me a few years ago because her child's class had used sand and minute particles had gotten onto her child's school jumper. Thankfully, it had not got into her tracheostomy tube, but I could understand the mother's concerns.

Our second qualified play therapist used art therapy in preference to sandplay. The term art therapy was coined by British artist, Adrian Hill in 1942 when recovering from tuberculosis. The British Association of Art Therapists (BAAT.org) runs regular 1-day art therapy introduction workshops and foundation courses.

Our play therapists tended to work 1–1 with students. Once we had qualified play therapists on our staff, we used Venture into Play (VIP) with groups of three students so that they got used to the social aspects of play. However, our VIP therapists did provide 1–1 if it was requested by teachers and certainly one little girl, Daisy, visited the VIP room at the start of each day to play with 'small world' toys. Once she had had her 'fix' she was able to go to her regular class and take part in lessons.

# Animal-assisted play therapy

Another type of play therapy that we used at our school was animal-assisted play therapy. We had a school dog that helped with the encouragement of play and playfulness for our students to aid them in expressing their feelings and developing relationships. If you decide to go down this route you will need a comprehensive public liability insurance in addition to a standard dog insurance. You will need to put policies in place beforehand and you will need the consent of the governing body. You will need to have a risk assessment in place. You will need to ensure that the dog is trained to be with children. It was highly successful for some of our students and to be honest some

*Figure 6.2 Animal-assisted play therapy*

of our staff found it therapeutic too. Views on this kind of therapy change all the time and so policies and risk assessments need to. To find out more go to www.dogstrustdogschool.org.uk

Lego® therapy is another play-based therapy that our students enjoyed. In the next chapter, we will find out more about how Lego and constructional play helped our students with executive functioning skills.

# Lego® and constructive play

## Constructive play

Constructive play is useful for students who may not be quite ready to move on to symbolic/fantasy play. Piaget belied that there were three stages of cognitive development and play and that constructive play was in the first stage (see Appendix 2). Many of the students that I have worked with have appeared to enjoy constructive play the most constructive play teaches children to be flexible thinkers (Bruner 1972). It tends to be goal oriented and requires focus and attention to avoid distractions and so could help develop executive functioning skills which many of our students find difficult. Our Lego club was usually attended by students in groups of three and this helped the students to gain the ability to interact and work with others to accomplish the joint goal. They learnt to negotiate, take the lead and move the group forward. Our Lego therapists fed back consistently by completing assessments and these showed that gains were made most often in language development and socialisation.

The central tenet of Seymour Papert's constructionist theory of learning is that people learn most effectively when they are actively engaged in constructing things. He became the first Lego professor of learning research in 1989. He is the genius brain behind Lego Mindstorms. He is one of my heroes.

I have to say that therapeutic Lego was the most sought after training from us of all the CPD training that we offered to other schools, including mainstream schools.

## Lego-Based Therapy®

Lego-based therapy was created by Daniel Legoff, a psychologist in the USA, after he noticed two children in his waiting room, playing together using their Lego sets.

During his weekly Lego-Based Therapy® with the two children, Legoff allocated specific joint and interactive jobs within the Lego building and got the children to take turns to carry out each role. He also provided a structured set of rules, giving the children responsibility for problem solving, using the rules as guidance. He found that the resulting interaction promoted the development of key skills including joint attention, sharing, collaboration, verbal and non-verbal communication and conflict resolution. The adult was able to take the role of facilitator, highlighting the presence of

DOI: 10.4324/9781003206538-7

any problems and encouraging pupils to come up with solutions. These experiences resulted in the children gaining a greater understanding of each other's points of view.

# Therapeutic Lego sessions

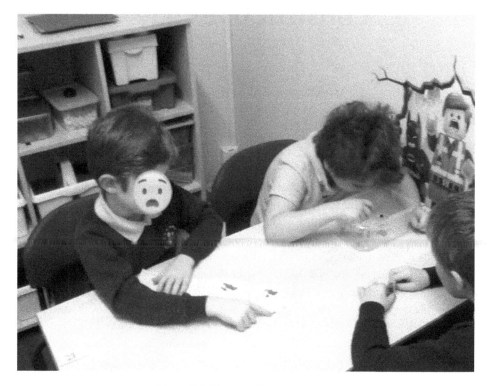

*Figure 7.1 Therapeutic Lego session*

Most of our students seemed naturally drawn to Lego. Students with Autism, ADHD or other learning difficulties often like rules, routine and structure and therapeutic Lego answered these needs.

At our school, there were three different levels of therapeutic Lego, Individual Lego – for one person, Collaboration Lego – pairs/two peers and Group Lego – for three peers.

Therapeutic Lego sessions in our school lasted for between 20 minutes and 40 minutes and were delivered once a week on the same day and at the same time. If you are going to introduce a therapy into your school it has to be timetabled and it cannot be stopped without preparing the student beforehand. If the member of staff is absent, then the student needs to be treated with respect and told in advance of when that session would be. If you have a behavioural incident because you did not deem it necessary, then you only have yourself to blame. Any therapeutic session is as important as a class lesson. In some instances, it is more important.

Students were prepared by a social story before their first session of therapeutic Lego took place. Lego rules were introduced to students participating for the first time. Rules and in-structions were visual.

For pupils taking part in therapeutic Lego sessions, parental consent should be sought, and each pupil should have a therapeutic Lego folder, with signed consent forms, attendance, communication placemats, IEPs, Annual Targets, school therapy and evaluation forms included, which are used throughout the block of sessions. Pupils communication placemats, IBPs and positive handling plans also need to be included within this folder.

Pupils should be allocated into one of the different levels by either the Lego therapist or class teacher. These levels are, Individual, Collaboration (Pairs/Two Peers) and Group (three peers). Checklists of skills at this level have been provided below. The formats, also below, should be followed depending on what level pupils have been assigned to. These formats should be displayed during the sessions. Visual timers in the form of sand timers, electronic timers, clocks or visual reminder cards should be used to support the pupils throughout the session.

# Suggestions for therapeutic Lego formats

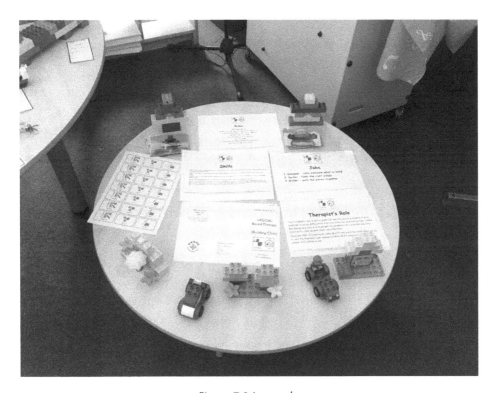

*Figure 7.2 Lego roles*

## *Individual format*

**20-minute sessions**

1.  Introduction **2 minutes** (greet and rules)

2. Pre-Building Skills **10 minutes** (pupils takes on the role of builder, working following skills – one skill each week)

   > **Role 1. Builder – finds and puts the Lego pieces together**

SKILLS

- Sorting by colour, shape and size
- Matching 3D pieces
- Matching 2D images (from instructions) with actual pieces
- Piece assembly
- Imitation
- Turn-taking
- Simple collaborative building

  *(only when every skill mastered above will you continue onto following)*

3. Building Skills **5 minutes** (small Lego kits with visual building plans provided – therapist and student taking it in turns to perform set roles)

   > **Role 1. Designer – tells everyone what to build**
   > **Role 2. Builder – finds and puts the Lego pieces together**

4. Tidy up **1 minute**
5. Circle time **2 minutes** (award completion certificate)


## Therapeutic Lego club session pairs and two peers format

**30-minute sessions**

1. Introduction **2 minutes** (greet and rules or set goals)
2. Lego set building **10 minutes** (small Lego kits with visual building plans provided – taking it in turns to perform set roles)

   > **Role 1. Designer – tells everyone what to build**
   > **Role 2. Builder – finds and puts the Lego pieces together**

3. Lego freestyle building **10 minutes** (pupils agree on a Lego project and build collaboratively, taking it in turns to perform set roles but without visual instruction sheets)
4. Tidy up **3 minutes**
5. Circle time **5 minutes** (showing Lego creations and certificates/prizes)

## Therapeutic Lego club session group format

**40-minute session**

1.  Introduction **2 minutes** (greet and rules or set goals)
2.  Lego set building **15 minutes** (small Lego kits with visual building plans provided – taking it in turns to perform set roles)

    - **Role 1. Designer – tells everyone what to build**
    - **Role 2. Sorter – finds the right Lego pieces**
    - **Role 3. Builder – puts the Lego pieces together**

3.  Lego freestyle building **15 minutes** (pupils agree on a Lego project and build collaboratively, taking it in turns to perform set roles but without visual instruction sheets)
4.  Tidy up **5 minutes**
5.  Circle time **3 minutes** (showing Lego creations and certificates/prizes)

During each session, children take it in turns to take on the following roles below. These roles/ jobs should be displayed during the session. (please see attached documents)

## Lego roles/Jobs

**Pairs**

- **Designer** – tells everyone what to build
- **Builder** – finds and puts the Lego pieces together

**Groups**

- **Designer** – tells everyone what to build
- **Sorter** – finds the right Lego pieces
- **Builder** – puts the Lego pieces together

During each therapy play session, the children are reminded of the following rules below. These rules should be displayed during the session (please see attached documents).

## Therapy play rules

- Clean up and put things back where they came from.
- Do not put Lego bricks in your mouth.
- Build things together!

- If you break it, you must fix it or ask for help to fix it.
- If someone else is using it, do not take it – ask first.
- Use indoor voices – no yelling.
- Keep your hands and feet to yourself.
- Use polite words.
- Clean up and put things back where they came from.

Sessions should always finish with circle time at the end to discuss and share the Lego creations. Over the course of the therapy play sessions, the following skills below are hoped to be demonstrated by the children.

- "Lego Helpers" are encouraged to help the group activities by pre-sorting pieces when set building, sorting freestyle pieces, checking sets against directions when completed, ordering and keeping the room tidy.
- "Lego Builders" can build small models in a group and design freestyle models with adult help and can competently fill each of the key roles in the set-building process – builder – sorter-designer.
- "Lego Creators" can build small models in groups and design freestyle models in pairs without adult help and can competently fill each of the key roles in the set-building process – builder – sorter-designer.
- "Lego Masters" can lead a large group project for which they then coordinate the construction or present to the group a desirable group freestyle project.
- "Lego Genius" can write a movie script or story which they present to the group. The script is then analysed by the group in terms of how the project can be translated into a Lego animated short film. The Lego master must lead the group in the project, including assigning building tasks for the set and characters, assigning action, voice, and sound-effects roles, controlling or assigning control of the camera and computer, and then directing the film itself. The project can take numerous sessions to complete.

Once the children can demonstrate one of the skills, they are given a certificate to reward their achievement in front of all the children at the end of the therapy session. They developed Lego brick building skills, including collaborative building as a team.

For students with multi-sensory problems, it may be necessary to develop play construction blocks that elicit an interesting tactile or auditory effect when manipulated, such as building blocks that play ascending notes on a musical scale when they are placed on top of each other in the correct order. Only specifically designed blocks that allow them to have manual control over the cause and effect of their actions and motivate the students by the auditory or tactile effect they elicit will stimulate them to play with building blocks. The Lego Braille Bricks kit was launched in August 2020 and was distributed free of charge to select institutions through participating partner networks in the markets where testing is being carried out with partners. If you have visually impaired students and wish to get involved, then visit http://www.Legobraillebricks.com

# The Lego play therapist's role

This therapy is a social play development programme, which is based on collaborative Lego play and promotes children working together to build Lego models in pairs and teams of three or more. It may be introduced gradually so that a student who finds playing alongside peers difficult learns how to take on each role with the therapist one to one to start with. It is argued that Lego therapy participants experience a greater motivation to initiate social contact and engage in sustained interactions with others (LeGoff 2004).

Remember that the therapist's role is *not* to point out specific social problems or give solutions to social difficulties that may arise during the session, rather the therapist's role is to highlight the presence of a problem and help children to come up with their own solutions.

Solutions that children have come up with are practised until they can do it, and the therapist can remind children of strategies in the future if similar difficulties arise.

Piaget's second stage of cognitive development and play is symbolic fantasy play or role-play. In the next chapter, we shall show how we can use role-play and enhance it with the use of virtual reality to support students with anxieties.

# Role-play

Piaget proposed that symbolic/fantasy play is the second stage of a child's cognitive development. Students with autism often find pretend play difficult but I have found that facilitated role-play (given the props, interactive support and script) that is consistent and predictable, in a designated area, can work.

Psychologists Leah Shefatya and Sara Smilansky worked together to propose that there are six developmental elements associated with role-play (Hendy & Toon 2001). These developmental stages (shown in Appendix 2) may need adapting in this digital age. They certainly do not make allowances for the continued development of role-playing that we engage in today, such as Cosplay.

## Cosplay

One summer we ran a Cosplay event at our school on a Saturday. I had met Giulietta Zawadzki alias Beau Peep, a well-known Cosplay artist, at a fundraising event in Edinburgh. She agreed to open the event for me. Students dressed as their favourite characters and Giulietta was one of our judges and she awarded prizes.

Schools everywhere have dressed up resources. It can be as basic as a dressing-up box in the early years where students get to act out as being Peppa Pig or Spiderman. It can be a wardrobe of historical costumes to help students appreciate a different period of time. New technology is allowing children to dress up in role-play using an avatar and in the near future, the metaverse will allow large-scale holograms linked to live and public events that will enable new layers of child-friendly role-play.

I think that the many superhero films and TV shows of characters that children like to watch have encouraged children with special needs to take part in role-playing. I know that whenever we had World Book Day in our primary special school the majority of our students would take part and would enjoy being their favourite character for the day. That was the reason for having the Cosplay event. Sometimes students knew everything there was to know about that character and had read every book about the character or had the books read to them. I have many students in mind as I write. Harry Potter was a particular favourite of some of our students.

DOI: 10.4324/9781003206538-8

Figure 8.1 Cosplay

Dr Who was another and one of our students, with autism, could quote scenes from Dr Who. Any opportunity to wear his favourite Dr Who costume and re-enact scenes helped him in developing social skills and he would often use a quote from Dr Who, using appropriate context, as a response to a situation that had arisen in the classroom. He seemed to have created scripts in his head from the TV programme to fit the many different scenarios he encountered in life.

Imaginative role-play can also help us to confront our demons. Sometimes it does not require that we dress up. There may instead be props that we can use or technology that can transport us into a role-playing situation.

## Play scripts

Vivian Gussin Paley (1991) was a pioneer of fantasy play. Encouraging young children to create their own stories that were then acted out in the classroom. Often students with severe learning difficulties have the cognitive age of infants or young children and so I believe her techniques are appropriate for children with special needs. Paley wrote "Let me study your play and figure out how play helps you solve your problems". She decided to deal with behaviour problems through writing scripts exchanging negative images for positive active roles wherever possible.

How can giving 'Time out' to a student with learning difficulties make them 'think about what they've done'? As Paley says "A child can no more think about social behaviour in the abstract than I can teach in the abstract. Children think by continuing to play and develop new roles".

She asks us to consider whether we view misbehaviour as 'bad' and therefore punishable or as the misreading of a script in progress. Remembering Shakespeare's line in As You Like It (1623) "All the world's a stage, and all the men and women merely players" she may indeed have been on to something. Goffman (1955) offers the idea that the interactions people have with one another on a daily basis are like a theatrical performance. I can certainly relate to that when teaching children with autism. In my experience some children with autism-like creating scripts in their heads and then find that they can use them at a later date when encountering a similar scenario. They do not always get it the right first time or even the second time. Allowing this practice instead of trying to stop them from being that character (which seems to act as a kind of protective shield) allows them to practice and develop social skills.

## Drama therapy

I am aware that drama therapy is well established in the Netherlands, UK and America. A fair percentage of drama therapists work in special education, forensics and various child, adolescent and adult mental health settings (Ihlen 2018). Therapeutic goals in drama therapy might be remedial action to improve mental and physical health whilst rehearsing desired behaviours and practising real-life situations through role-play.

A pilot investigation was undertaken this century into the use of drama therapy using the SENSE theatre project to improve socioemotional functioning and reduce stress in children with ASD. The investigation included the use of measuring cortisol and oxytocin levels throughout the pilot. It included neuropsychological and behavioural parent-report measures. All of these measures were analysed. The report concluded that the use of therapeutic drama techniques showed potential promise (Corbett BA 2010). In 2014, a further study was carried out that corroborated the findings (Corbett 2014).

Role-play allows us to practice stressful situations in a safe, nurturing environment. I have used drama and role-play to great effect with teenagers in a special school where we acted out our own version of Romeo and Juliet. Students were able to discuss what they thought of being in love. It allowed them the freedom to talk about teenage issues that concerned them. It was not a drama lesson in the traditional sense of understanding Shakespeare, which is difficult enough for an ordinary teenager to do but it was using Shakespeare as a vehicle for them to recognise their own emotions. Films, cartoons, even the ballet of the play would be shared with the students to really immerse them in the experience.

I remember acting out the battle between the Capulets and Montagues with 8 years old in a different special school to the music used in the Apprentice (a TV programme) and taken from the Dance of the Knights in Prokofiev's ballet, Romeo and Juliet. It was a useful inroad for the boys in helping them to control their emotions. Researchers examined the effects of a play intervention on pre-schoolers with social delays (Craig-Unkefer and Kaiser 2003). The researchers used role-play (e.g., playing doctor), dramatic play (e.g., playing dress up) to successfully increase social-communicative interactions.

## Surplus reality

Theory of mind (ToM) is a popular term from the field of psychology used to describe being able to put oneself in someone else's shoes. Students in special schools are often unable to do this due to their learning differences. Sometimes our students need the guided support Paley offered (1991) by turning children's news stories or worries into role-play in order for them to better understand these situations.

Children with autism, ADHD and other complex needs can have phobias and fears about real-life situations. It is important for parents and teachers to know how to prepare students for those situations. Z.T. Moreno, co-founder of the psychotherapy method, known as psychodrama coined the term surplus reality. Surplus reality is a kind of alternative reality, a shared social space where a group can act out or rehearse painful situations or relationships from a partici-pant's life. A safe way to experience reality.

Marvin Minsky's (1975) frame system theory suggests that whenever we encounter a new situation (or have to change one's view) we select from memory a structure called a frame. This is a remembered framework to be adapted to fit the new reality by changing details, as ne-cessary. Frame analysis can be defined as the study of the cognitive organisation of social experiences. It is this recognition of a framework or schema that I believe some students with autism have difficulty with and I believe immersive virtual reality (VR) can help. Goffman (1974) believed that frames organise experiences and help us to decipher what is happening around us.

# Virtual reality and role-play

When I worked in schools it worried me that some students were fearful of going to the dentists, the hairdressers and other places.

Students with learning differences often find real-life situations difficult experiences. How often has a parent of a young child with such challenges stood by helplessly as their child has a meltdown in a supermarket, at a road crossing on a train? How could we use a combination of role-play and modern-day technology to make real-life situations easier for them? I researched the issue and found that Haifa University in Israel had done some ground-breaking work using virtual reality with students who had autism (Josman & Weis 2008). The solution as I saw it was to recreate these places that caused concern through VR in a safe environment with the support of experienced adults. We found that VR role-play can help reduce anxieties and prepare students for real-life situations that they fear the most.

Many of our students would not tolerate wearing a VR headset and so we set up an immersive interaction room at Ysgol Pen Coch in the summer recess of 2016 using OMI Interactive (Visit their website at http://www.Omi.uk for more information) funded by our parents association. Omi does not specialise in providing these situations. They provide the equipment. They will train your staff in using the technology so that you can produce the scenarios that meet the needs of your students. The immersive room experience is very real. It allows students to experience and play out difficult situations that they often meet during their daily life. Virtual reality allows a student to explore and experience situations as if they were actually present in that environment or place.

We found that students who experience virtual reality are able to carry out specific activities with significantly increased confidence. We found the impact of virtual reality on students' ability to cope when in a fight, flight, freeze or appease situation has led to real-life functional improvements for activities that were previously not possible. This has had a significant impact on students' readiness to learn, their wellbeing and engagement. Sometimes the impact was qualitative and sometimes it was quantitative. Learning is qualitatively and quantitatively better if learners are given the opportunity to immerse in the situation they are trying to understand and learn from.

Parents and teachers have watched children with autism play back a scene in a movie over and over again to help them make sense of a confusing world. Using that knowledge, we re-created virtual reality situations of importance to our students.

# The immersive VR room

We introduced a room that children with autism could enter, press a switch and the room became an immersive 360° room. Safe and secure with a trusted teaching assistant the student could play back that scene/scenes as many times as they wished until they felt comfortable enough to visit its real counterpart.

It became hugely successful and continues to be used today giving students a 360° experience. Virtual Reality is by its very nature a visual-oriented experience. Many of the students we taught are thought to be visual learners. "Children with autism rarely have opportunities to experience or to learn to cope with day-to-day situations. Using virtual simulations enables them to acquire skills that will make it possible for them to become independent" (Josman & Weis 2008).

The setting up of this room enabled us to be able to offer our students the chance to experience and play out difficult situations which they often met during their daily life and routine. Equipped with floor-to-ceiling screens displaying projected video footage, as well as surround sound, lighting and interactive walls, the room engaged students in a complete sensory experience and gave students a feeling of total immersion. The room almost completely filtered out interference from outside the room thus allowing the student to focus entirely on the virtual environment. This was far more intensive than role-play by itself. If you have tried out VR you will know that you have become that character in the immersive experience.

Handheld controllers and sensors gave a whole new feel to the artificial reality experience. Transmitters and receivers on the walls enabled an immersive experience that was very real. This is not simply an engagement tool or a gimmick, it allows a student to explore and to experience as if they are actually present in that environment or place. I have written in detail about this in my book on VR, AR and AI in Special Education (Anderson 2019).

Our staff visited the places on the list and took various photographs and made a recording of all the sounds experienced at those places. They were then transferred onto a programme on the computer which is connected to the immersive equipment thus creating a VR experience. This resulted in 3D version of the places that caused concern being projected onto three walls in the room. Beams of light project large, coloured spots onto the floor of the room. Each has an image attached, along with an accompanying sound where relevant. These are activated by passing a disc or wand across the appropriate colour to break the beam.

Each student, whom it, was felt would benefit from this extra interaction was offered an individual session of between 10 and 15 minutes in length once a week spanning over a period of 8 weeks in total and split up into 3 stages. During this time each student was encouraged to act out a scenario worked out by staff (sometimes with parent input).

Once the children were confident with the first stage of the experience, they moved onto the second stage still in the virtual reality room.

Using role-play props that a student may come across in that setting the student would act out the drama that caused them concern. An experienced adult would be there to ensure that the experience ended before the student got upset and the time would gradually get longer until the student felt completely comfortable in that situation.

At third stage, students were taken to the actual place to see whether the extra input throughout these sessions had been successful or not in helping them to cope with the situation that had caused them concern.

This is often what drama/role-play is all about in a special school. It may not be what you would expect the drama to be in a mainstream school.

Helen, a HLTA at the school, was passionate about the use of the VR room to support students with autism. Omi employed her at National Autism Conferences to show attendees how the VR room did that for our students.

A study by The University of Texas at Dallas in the USA showed that virtual reality training programmes produced positive results. "The virtual reality training platform creates a safe place for participants to practice social situations without the intense fear of consequence" (Dr Nyaz Didehbani 2016). The finding was published in the Journal Computers in Human Behaviour.

## Success stories

The virtual reality room was used for an individual student with autism whose parents had to do a two-mile detour every day to bring him to school so that they did not have to go through traffic lights. He was very agitated in the car and screamed if they came upon a traffic light during a car ride. The situation was recreated in the virtual reality room and the student was able to operate the traffic lights for himself. After two weeks of daily visits to the room, the parents were able to report that they no longer had to avoid traffic lights. Their child no longer has an issue with traffic lights and was perfectly content in the car. An added bonus was that they could leave home at a reasonable time. The student had learnt, through role-play and VR, how to self-regulate his behaviour.

The room was used to successfully teach 30 students to use a road crossing. The room also became the dental surgery that the majority of our students attended. One of our students with severe autism just could not cope with going there. She visited it in our VR room. We were given replica props by the dental support team. She attended the make believe surgery regularly for 6 weeks and then mum took her to the actual dentist. She had a successful visit and continued to attend the dentist surgery with no problem. We repeated this for other students that the dentist flagged up. The dental team praised us at an annual meeting and told me that they no longer had problems with any of our students attending the dentist surgery and that this was unheard of in the past.

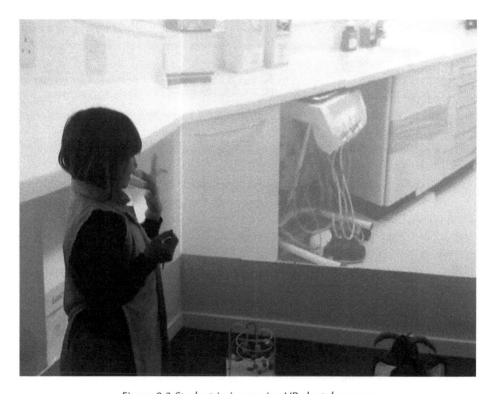

*Figure 8.2 Student in immersive VR dental surgery*

# Episodic memory

Using VR can be seen as a kind of scaffolding as we prepare our students to succeed in the real world by practising skills in the VR world. I would argue that it can develop episodic memory – a term coined by neuroscientist Endel Tulving. Episodic memory allows us to use our imagination to revisit events. I believe that VR allows us to create successful visits to these places and that it creates causal knowledge in our students so that every time they enter the VR room and successfully visit the place that used to cause them distress, they are instead creating a counterfactual thought where the visit is successful. Once they have built up a memory bank of successful visits, they are ready to visit in the real world. There is extensive evidence suggesting that both adults and children can use causal models in this way to make predictions and design interventions (Buchsbaum et al. 2012). Buchsbaum argues that role-play lets children practise the cognitive skills necessary for causal learning, planning and counterfactual reasoning. I believe that the success that we have had with using the VR room and props in this way backs up that argument. Ginsburg et al. (2011) maintain that 'even small children use imaginative play and fantasy play to take on their fears and create or explore a world they can master'. Ginsburg goes on to suggest that sensitive adults can observe this role play to recognise the fears that need to be addressed and that role-play helps children to 'develop new competencies that lead to enhanced confidence and the resilience needed to address future challenges'.

# A safe environment

The use of virtual reality to create a controlled and safe environment that is closely representative of real-life has proven beneficial to students in our care. We all learn by seeing and watching. Students who suffer from fears and phobias are now able to build their own private secure library of how to cope with social situations that ordinary students take for granted. VR is proving to be an effective tool for the school in enhancing social skills and social cognition in students with autism and ADHD.

We also found the VR room was ideal for those students with physical disabilities providing them with the opportunity to experience things they may not be able to physically access. Our VR room enabled us to present information such as video footage, 360° panoramic views of places such as the airport, the dentist, the supermarket, their future secondary school, the local area and exotic holiday places.

# Training

The training on using the high resolution 360° Ricoh Theta camera took fifteen minutes. It has spherical still images and 4K video as well as 360° spatial audio recordings. A spherical image was taken immediately in one shot and was then edited and shared with us in a minute. The camera enabled us to create our own virtual tours both for the VR headsets we owned and for our VR room. It allowed us to share our creations with parents. If we created a virtual tour of a supermarket, for instance, to support students who find going into supermarkets difficult then parents could also take their child through the tour at home on a tablet or iPad.

The THETA can be remotely connected to a smartphone. VR technology had been available since the mid 20th century, but it is only now relatively affordable for schools. Traditional forms of teaching do not suit students with learning disabilities. Our students with learning disabilities have made progress through the use of VR mainly because it can turn a passive learning experience into an active one.

In the next chapter, we shall examine the use of technology in play further as we investigate the benefits of digital play for students who had limited opportunities to play before the dawn of technology.

# 9 Digital play

Today's play includes online and offline environments. Media influence and the latest technologies actively encourage everyone, from the youngest to the oldest in society to use virtual and non-virtual domains for play, entertainment and recreation. With exponential access to digital media, children's play worlds are expanding. They can connect with peers in new ways using interactive and immersive technology. I danced along to records with my siblings when I was a child. Records that my parents chose and could afford. They were few. Today children can tell Alexa to play anything that appeals to them, to dance or sing along to. In the near future, they may even dance alongside the holograms of their idol. Play today, in this technological age, has moved on and changed forever.

The technological revolution has given students with severe or profound learning difficulties opportunities to play that they never had in the past.

## Digital competence framework

Countries all over the world have updated their school curriculums in light of the changing world we live in. As the headteacher of a Pioneer school, we led other schools in Wales on taking the new curriculum forward. In the new curriculum, there is a strong focus on digital competence. Digital competence is different from ICT skills. Digital competence is the development of digital skills across the curriculum, preparing students for the opportunities and risks that an online world presents.

Advances in technology and globalisation have transformed the way we live and work. These changes have profound implications for what, and how, children and young people learn. After all, tablets and smartphones did not even exist when the last curriculum was introduced in 1993. In 2017, I found that the draft digital framework showed just how good our students were in an area that they had not been given appropriate assessment for in the past. It was the school staff who struggled. Some openly admitted to having the biggest learning curve in delivering and assessing digital competence.

Burke and Marsh (2013) consider the way children's digital play is supported and fostered by family members who recognise the potential such play offers, whilst being alert to its challenges.

DOI: 10.4324/9781003206538-9

Other play proponents actively discourage digital play in favour of free play (Sahlberg & Doyle 2019). I believe that all types of play are important. In fact, I would say that play is just being redefined by new innovations in technology. Not all children are the same and some children, particularly those with disabilities, require digital play or technology in order to play.

# Engagement through technology

Students with severe or profound learning disabilities can have difficulty with accessing video games. A charity (https://specialeffect.org.uk) supplies adapted technology to people with severe disabilities, which allows them to access communication tools and play video games on a level playing field. Being able to play is therapeutic and digital play is highly motivating for some students with severe physical challenges. The controllers will use any part of the body from a small toe movement to a player's eye gaze. The charity has free Eyemine software that helps students who have an eye gaze machine the freedom to play Minecraft. The opportunity to play games can improve the mental health of players. If you were to search on Twitter for disability play you would find many tweets from disabled people who have found digital play a lifesaver. Before they had access to digital games, they often felt helpless and without hope. Contact the charity if you have a child who could benefit. They do not charge anything. They will assess the person. They will loan the equipment. The person will stay on their books and equipment needs are constantly monitored and updated to meet the changing needs of the person. They will even meet your child in intensive care to give access to games.

When it comes to digital games themselves, students need to be able to figure out the rules, hints and tips before they can start playing. I do not know how some of my students have done this, but they have. So, did they teach themselves to read? Once the rules have been read and the game loaded the students' imagination takes over as they begin to play the game. Players often accept the rules of the game just because they make the activity of the game possible. In the game, they take risks and learn from their mistakes. This is quite a learning experience. Games may teach lessons in strategy and mastery. They allow students to inhabit different perspectives as they take on the role play of characters and interact in the game. This is learning through play. Students often do not realise that they are learning.

Seymour Papert once said *"Every maker of video games knows something that the makers of curriculum don't seem to understand. You'll never see a video game being advertised as being easy. Kids who do not like school will tell you it's not because it's too hard. It's because it's boring"*.

So how can we harness the obvious pulling power of technological play into the classroom so that students learn without feeling they are being taught. Papert also once predicted that schools would change and that *"the ultimate pressure for change will be child power"*.

I have seen boys with autism and ADHD who seem to struggle with numeracy and literacy fly through a PlayStation game deemed too old for them. How do they manage that? The PlayStation certainly improved their focus and engagement. If you are a gamer and have ever played a video game before, you know that it can take a long time to figure out the PlayStation game rules. You need to be able to read to get all the information necessary to play your favourite game. What an incentive to learn to read! There are now schools that teach only through playing online games. The Institute of Play is one such school. It is based in New York.

I noticed many years ago that students with autism in my class did not like the close contact of reading but enjoyed observing print from a distance and easily spotted the MacDonald's sign when out on a trip. We purchased the Oxford Tree online reading books and put them on the white boards in all the classrooms. I did the same in my last school. Students with autism enjoyed the interactive opportunities as well as being able to be at a distance from the board. I witnessed many who had taught themselves to read in this way. They did not feel threatened and so it was no longer a task but something that was fun.

I do believe that children are showing us that the way to engage them is through technology. This has been true for all the children that I have taught in special schools in recent years. From students with PMLD who enjoy using the eye gaze in order to play a game to a student with Asperger teaching himself coding skills and creating an animation project. Children are born into this age of technology and seem more at home with it than many adults.

Using the right kind of technology can support students learning and skills. For those students who have fine motor skill development issues as part of their diagnosis no amount of making them trace over words is going to encourage them to do something that is difficult for them. Give them a technological tool that enables them to communicate their ideas and you have gained their trust and given them the opportunity to make progress.

Sometimes students with autism find it difficult to perform in front of others and I have watched students close their eyes or turn their back to audiences when performing in the real world. The internet has given these students the opportunity to perform in front of others without the need to see their reactions.

# The effects of the Covid pandemic

The pandemic meant that children could not meet with friends at the local sports field to kick a ball around. Many students that attend special schools have severe disabilities that mean they are unable to join in those games anyhow. Most students that attend special schools travel by minibus to school and do not have friends who live nearby. But at least those that were able to could meet online and play together. The pandemic shifted culture online.

A few of our young students during the pandemic connected through games with friends or siblings, playing Minecraft together on the same console. Gaming devices such as the Nintendo Wii and Nintendo DSi also offer online play. These types of games encourage abstract thinking. They involve fantasy play as on screen avatars which Piaget rated as the second stage of cognitive development. A stage we might be surprised to find some students with SLD find so easy through digital engagement. Why do they find it so easy when they have to reorganise images and ideas from their own minds in order to take part in these online play worlds? In digital play, children are expected to upload content – images, recordings, messages, animations and take part in teamwork and negotiations. Digital play suspends reality and develops cognition. It would appear that a desire to learn to play online successfully can develop these learning skills.

During the Covid pandemic, some parents have hosted their children's parties inside platforms such as Roblox. It is a context that makes sense in the world we now live in. I have seen great party bag presents that include blue light glasses. Considering the amount of screen usage by our children in this 21st century I think those parents got it spot on.

# Collaboration between home and school

I have worked in schools for many years. I have noticed that sometimes communication between home and school about a child's use of technology – as an object of play as well as an aid to learning (in both settings) – is not discussed or seen as important. In this technology-driven age believe that needs to change. In the past schools were expected to teach the children the three Rs when they entered the school and most parents left them to it. Today many parents use technology with their children almost as soon as they are born. They monitor their sleep and support it with the use of AI. They allow their toddlers the use of the phone to keep them occupied whilst waiting in a queue. Many homes have technological equipment in the kitchen, have Alexa, Cortana or Siri in different rooms and augmented reality books to keep their children's interest. Children ask Alexa and Google anything they wish to know. PlayStation and VR are commonplace, as are other technological games in homes today. Children have access to tablets and apps in the home. When children enter school and become students, they sometimes must manage without the technological aids that they were used to using in the home. But why should they?

Schools have had to become more digital savvy during the coronavirus pandemic and have had to work with families on delivering the curriculum online in student's homes. The pandemic has shown us that it is necessary for schools to request information on what technology and what apps they have used in the home. In order for schools to know how to support them during the pandemic. School and home should be a partnership. Arguably no one knows a child as well as its parents. It could also be useful for parents/carers to use the school as a support mechanism in this digital age. I remember a parent coming to see me in 2016. She had, the night before, discovered her daughter, aged nine, still playing on her X box in her bedroom at 10 pm. She was not alone. She was playing with remote friends. They were all adult males. It is good practice for schools to offer awareness training for parents. In my book, Virtual Reality, Augmented Reality and Artificial intelligence in Special Education (2019) I include a chapter on this important topic.

I am reminded of a student volunteer who was deaf and supported our technician at a special school where I was an assistant head. He told me one day that he enjoyed playing online games because no one would judge him on his disability because they did not know he had one.

A UK Survey Data formed part of Children, Technology and Play (2019–2020), an 8-month co-produced study by academics from the University of Sheffield and University of Cape Town, South Africa, the Lego Foundation and Dubit (researchers in digital entertainment for children). This study has given us some interesting information that back up my beliefs and experience. Below is a table adapted from the report http://techandplay.org/download-report that shows skills that young children are capable of when using the tablet for an average of 1 hour 19 minutes weekdays and 1 hour 23 minutes on weekends.

**A comparison of what skills 0–2s and 3–5s use unassisted when playing with a tablet (as reported by parents).**

| Unassisted skill development when playing with a tablet | 0–2yrs | 3–5yrs |
|---|---|---|
| Swipe the screen (e.g., to change photos, turn the 'page' of an e-book) | 54% | 76% |
| Trace shapes with their fingers | 44% | 75% |
| Drag items across the screen | 45% | 72% |
| Open their apps | 44% | 75% |
| Draw things | 43% | 73% |
| Tap the screen to operate commands | 43% | 72% |
| Exit apps and enter other apps | 40% | 69% |
| Drag items and trace shapes | 36% | 69% |
| Turn the device on and off | 40% | 66% |
| Increase or decrease the volume | 33% | 65% |
| Use learning apps | 32% | 64% |
| Unlock the device | 37% | 58% |
| Use creativity apps | 32% | 61% |
| Take photos | 33% | 60% |
| Click on a cross in a box to get rid of a pop-up | 28% | 59% |
| Use gaming apps | 28% | 56% |
| Enlarge or decrease the size of objects by pinching and dragging | 25% | 50% |
| Show others e.g., siblings how to use the device | 23% | 50% |
| Use video apps | 25% | 44% |
| Use reading apps | 18% | 40% |
| Make videos | 15% | 22% |
| Find new apps in the app-store/market place | 14% | 24% |
| Purchase new apps in the app-store/market place | 13% | 16% |

We have probably all sat next to someone at an airport or Drs surgery where a tablet has been given to the infant as a distraction technique and the survey bears this out. Vygotsky said, "The child not only masters the items of cultural experience but the habits and forms of cultural behaviour" (Vygotsky 1929).

The survey highlights its use for encouraging creativity and play as well as supporting learning and education. Most of the time the decision to use the tablet was solely or mainly that of the parents. This supports my suggestion that work needs to be done between schools and parents to have a clearer assessment of a child's technological competence as soon as they start school.

The survey showed that the most important features for apps parents downloaded were that they were fun, easy to use and educational. Parent's favourite apps were related to learning whilst children's favourite apps were about play and creativity.

# The future is technology

The survey showed that young children, before they start school, use a tablet to play games, look after virtual pets, create virtual worlds and dress up avatars as they take the leap into immersive worlds that now can include digital scent technology to add to the sensory experience. Minecraft Earth is the augmented reality game that lets children go on exciting adventures, build something with friends online and then step into life-size creations. They can draw and paint on the tablet without the need for paint or crayons.

If we observe students with limited gross motor and manual abilities, we can see that they have fewer opportunities to engage in free play. In an investigation led by Rios-Rincon et al. (2016), it was found that using robotic interventions for children with limitations in motor abilities increased their level of playfulness.

New technologies are providing new ways to engage, inspire and educate children through immersive play trends. They use augmented reality to bridge the physical and digital worlds. Digital content is used to extend and sustain engagement with physical toys. Voice-driven play with new digital facilitators scaffolds the learning experience and inspire playtime. Next-generation voice assistants (powered by AI) support teachers and parents whilst supporting the child. Traditional passive TV viewing is being transformed with interactive experiences being delivered via the cloud. The development of AI allows children to immerse themselves with the characters in storybooks.

New technologies are catalysing new ways to play. Blurred lines between the digital and physical world are commonplace for our students before they even enter school. High-speed networks enable real-time interactivity. Our perception of technology in schools needs to change to see it as a medium that facilitates playtime so that our students can harness technology to become creators and storytellers. Never before has learning through play been so accessible to students with learning differences as it is today.

I am hopeful that the digital competence frameworks that countries are introducing into schools will ensure a future where students with learning differences find it easier to learn to play and learn to learn than ever before.

In the next chapter, we shall look at how we can support parents with ensuring their children get as much access to play opportunities as possible.

# Parents and play

We are all products of our own upbringing. This means that we have developed our own ways of interacting with others according to that upbringing. We need to be aware of these when interacting with our children as we encourage them to develop play skills, particularly if they have learning difficulties. Children with severe or profound learning difficulties require lots and lots of repetition in the sensorimotor stage of play to enable them to move on. They may be unable to play by themselves and need to be guided play or supportive play and they should enjoy this if we interact effectively.

Is the way we interact working for them? Do we need to change so that we meet their needs better? It is important to find out what they prefer to play and join them in their preferred play. It is important to help them to learn how to play and to take turns. As adult, it is our responsibility to do this in a non-threatening, playful approach so that they become able to develop those play skills and want to play with us again and again. How we play will affect our child. If we observe how it affects our child, we should begin to understand the effect of our own behaviour on our child. If we lose patience, they may pick up on this. We may choose to lighten the mood so that our anxiety and tension disappears. Our child will pick up on these nonverbal cues of a state of calm and should begin to trust and respect our responses. They may learn to share and cooperate if we share and cooperate. Developing play skills is the precursor to developing learning skills. A calm, loving family member would always be a child's first choice when selecting a play companion.

Technology today may support your child in their development of play skills. In 2010 a parent came to see me in school as she wanted her child to have access to the new Tobii eye-pointing technology in school. We already used E-Tran frames in school, which are Perspex see through frames that you can attach symbols, letters, pictures or words to for the child to eye point to and communicate their needs and wants. It is useful for children with severe motor and physical needs that prevent them from signing or speaking. I was keen for her daughter to have the opportunity of using eye gaze technology and approached the local authority for funding. They insisted that the speech and language therapy service (SaLT) assess her daughter for suitability. The company visited the school with the equipment and in front of a group of professionals from the local authority and representatives from the SaLT team, the little girl was expected to perform. She was, and still is, a sensitive soul and could not 'perform' on demand. The local authority, on the advice of their

DOI: 10.4324/9781003206538-10

professionals and the speech therapists who attended the demonstration, refused to fund it. Speech therapists recommended that she persevere with the E-Tran frame. There is nothing wrong with E-Tran frames. Johnathan Bryan, an author, was diagnosed with PMLD yet was taught to read and write using an E-Tran frame. Johnathan wrote in his book *Eye Can Write (2018)* that although he knew himself that he did not have PMLD he did have profound and multiple difficulties in accessing learning. He prefers to use the E-Tran frame to an eye gaze machine. Please visit www.teachustoo.org.uk to find out more about Johnathan and his charity.

The parent at my school did not believe the E-Tran frame was the only answer. She managed to get a charity to fund an eye gaze machine for her daughter at home. She taught her child to use it. She then loaned it to school so that we could use it with her daughter. I managed to find funding to get one for school and many students have benefitted from the use of eye gaze. One student, previously diagnosed with PMLD progressed rapidly through the use of the eye gaze machine and proved that it was indeed his access to learning that was the problem not his ability. Eye gaze is successful in that it can allow students to communicate but it also provides many games for them to play. For students with limited mobility, play can seem limited too. The eye gaze allows them to play. Please see the digital play chapter for more ideas on using eye gaze for play. https://www.stevemorganfoundation.org.uk will support funding in North Wales, Merseyside and Cheshire and funded many projects at our school, including individual family projects. https://www.getgrants.org.uk will support you in finding grants. https://www.baileythomas.org.uk offers grants for families affected by disabilities.

Some parents worry about what kinds of things to play with a child with disabilities. Other parents choose to include their child in everything. It is worth bearing in mind what the disability is and then finding play activities that they might enjoy. The earlier you start to offer to play the sooner you find out what play they respond to.

There are chapters in this book that parents may wish to copy ideas from. Creating a sensory profile of your child will help you immensely when deciding on appropriate games. There is a template for a sensory profile in the resource chapter of this book.

# Play opportunities and ideas

If your child is unable to move because of their disability, then hiding your face behind your hands is a good start. During the Covid pandemic, we had to hide our faces behind a mask, and this actually helps your child to identify your voice or nuances so that they still feel secure and know it is you. They are mastering the concept of you disappearing and coming back. Often, we worry when leaving a child for the first time, perhaps it is with a relative, at a nursery or even the hospital. I remember one of our students with PMLD, aged six, who had separation anxiety. Hide and seek and Peekaboo are good games for helping a child to realise that you will come back. The sooner you start this play and consistently repeat it the more you will help your child cope with separation anxiety. Any play that helps them learn that you will return is a good game. This helps to build a schema in the brain, but it takes a lot of repetition. You will know when you have succeeded in building that schema. They will not cry when they immediately lose sight of you. If you manage to build a repertoire of games to play with your child that they enjoy then share them with other family members and go out of the room or house for short periods. They will be able to forge playtimes with others and learn that you will return.

If your child needs to sit in a wheelchair for a while and the chair has a tray that can be attached, then putting sensory toys on the tray may encourage your child to touch them. By observing your child, you may see which toy they favour. If they manage to throw a toy on the floor and hopefully you pick it up, they are developing an understanding of cause and effect. "If I throw this toy my parent will pick it up". This is quite a cognitive skill and deserves encouragement. If you tired of it let someone else take over if your child is still enjoying it. This is a game that your child may enjoy for years, and you are making them feel secure by its repetition and familiarity. You are also creating a bond.

Once your child has mastered throwing items from their chair you can move on to throw and catch. This teaches cause and effect as well as hand-eye coordination. It also teaches that you will respond to their actions. A soft ball, small soft teddy or bean bag is always something worth keeping in your child's play sack as safe throwing toys. If a child really likes a specific toy, it is sometimes worth buying more than one. If they were to lose the only one they had, they, and you, may have sleepless nights. Sometimes parents sent their 3rd copy of the toy to school so that it could be used if their child became anxious. Sometimes parents bought variations of the same toy to teach their child the concept of the same but different.

In special schools, we use songs and music daily for transition and these can be shared with parents. If you can sing to your child as you do mundane tasks you may make your child laugh. If you use the same songs and music for certain transition times of the day it creates a routine, familiarity and security and teaches a sense of time.

I have already written about the benefits of swings and trampolines in this book, and it is possible to buy both for use at home too.

I remember being sent some great photos from a family of a teenager with PMLD. They had covered the lounge floor in an old sheet and left trays of paint for their son, Matthew, to play with. The sheer joy on his face just showed me how well his family understood his love of painting. Matthew enjoyed a lovely relaxing bath at the end of the activity whilst the room was restored in time for his favourite TV programme.

It is great when parents share successful play activities that they use at home. Parents of a student who had severe autism shared with us his love of water. This was great for us, as when he needed to decompress, staff would take him outside to the water area where he could get soaked. He enjoyed the activity and his parents were glad his sensory needs were being met.

Even getting dressed can become a playful opportunity. Just because your child may have been diagnosed with a disability, or you may suspect they are not understanding as well as their siblings or peers, you can still make it fun. Naming items of clothing in funny voices as you put them on is an example one parent shared with me. Once you have repeated this routine many times you may decide to swap the names for items that do not make sense to see if your child realises what you have done. Make it fun, do not pressurise and remember to give your child time to process what you have said. Any daily chore can become playful if you make it a game, even brushing teeth. Doing things in a playful way engages children more and strengthens the parent–child bond.

In this book, we looked at DIR floortime used in school, but it can also be used at home. In fact, you can copy any of the suggestions in this book at home. Theraplay is similar in parts to

DIR as it is developmental. It supports families in developing strong families through play. To find out more go to http://theraplay.org

Filial therapy is family therapy using play therapy methods and the filial play coaching course has been clinically accredited by PTUK. It is designed to improve parent/child relationships. A play therapist trains and supervises parents in their own home to have special therapeutic play time sessions with their children. Filial therapy usually takes from 18 to 24 weeks to complete. To find out more go to http://playtherapy.org.uk

## School support for parents

Many schools, ours included offer support for parents. As soon as the school opened, I set up a Bubbles hydrotherapy group for parents of babies and toddlers with severe or profound disabilities. They could come with their child to play with their child in the pool under guidance from our pool manager. The pool was separated from the main body of the school so they did not feel pressured that their child would be expected to attend our school when they reached school age. It gave those parents a chance to learn how to play in the pool with their child and meet other parents of children with disabilities.

I also set up a parent partnership where parents could come to school for training in Makaton, behaviour management, etc. as well as attend craft days with their children. We also provided support for their own health and wellbeing. They could attend any therapeutic play sessions to find out more about them to see if they wished to request them for their child in school and copy ideas for use at home.

Parent partnership was successful for those parents who did not work. Some parents took advantage of knowing that their child was safe in school to get a paid job and so were unable to attend in person. We began putting training and support online. We provided videos. We also created online secure parent access to all documents sent home as well as copies of Annual Reviews, IEPs and IBPs. We provided up-to-date information on how their child was getting on in school. Like a lot of schools, we also developed a Twitter account with up-to-date photos of the fun their child was having that day.

## Play, leisure pursuits and residentials

Play is important whatever our students age. I remember some years ago taking some teenagers with PMLD to Alton Towers theme park. As any parent with a child with disabilities knows you can go to the front of the queue in theme parks if you have a child with a disability. We had been given bracelet passes to allow us to the front of the queue. It was in the 1990s before written risk assessments, written weeks in advance, consumed us. We risk assessed it on the spot. We were well staffed. I remember we somehow got 3 of our boys, normally in wheelchairs, onto the log flume. They seemed to enjoy every second of it. There was plenty of laughter and smiles and no signs of fear on their faces. They were well protected from the water cascades with disposable plastic capes. Were we wrong to give them that opportunity? I do not think so, but I do wish that these sort of places made these experiences available and easily accessible to all. What makes anyone think that they would not enjoy the experience that ordinary teenagers take for granted? Legoland is another theme park certainly worth the visit if it is not too far from your school or home for a day trip. Particularly if your child enjoys playing with Lego or has Lego therapy at school.

On another occasion during the early 1990s, we took our students to Dan yr Ogof caves. My sister, also a teacher at the time, was enthused about the caves for her 4 years old reception students and she felt it was ideal for my students. I think she just forgot that some of my 16 years old students with PMLD were in wheelchairs. In hindsight, it was not ideal in parts for wheelchair users at that time and so we could not visit every part of the caves, but we could visit most. The students loved the experience and in one area of the caves where the ceilings get very low one of our students found he could hear his echoes and so made the most noise we had ever heard him make. It is great to take children with disabilities on as many leisure pursuits as possible, but you must ensure the site has risk assessments and that you have changing facilities available, or you equip your transport with these facilities.

Sometimes we would take our students away for the school week. It was a week of leisure and play pursuits for the students but a daunting undertaking for staff. A huge amount of preparation goes into one of these residential trips. Risk assessments are vital. Visits beforehand to the chosen residential centre are essential. Rota systems for night duties are essential. Safeguarding and health and safety risks have to be considered. Timetables for the week have to be drawn up beforehand and chosen visits, entrance fees, food, changing places, etc. all have to be taken into the account and approved of by the school senior management team. Many parents support these residentials. Parents sometimes accompanied us as volunteer helpers. Your local authority will have policies with regard to offsite visits that you will need to comply with. I also recommend that the school has robust school policies in place beforehand. There is no point in listing the places we visited in this book as these places change constantly and a google search will provide you with the most up-to-date residential facilities for students with learning differences or disabilities.

Sometimes individual risk assessments are necessary if you are unsure about the safety of a particular student or, indeed if taking a student impacts upon the safety of the other students on a residential or day trip. Sometimes parents want their child to have the opportunity whatever the cost. Sometimes parents need respite. Sometimes parents are scared to give their children the opportunity. Risk assessments will reassure parents about the school's decision. I recall in one school that a teacher decided he was taking a certain student away for the week regardless of staff concerns. His class made the local tv news as the student concerned decided that he was going to stay in the sea for hours and rescue helicopters were sent out to return him to safety.

Sometimes it can be difficult for families to fund holidays for their child with disabilities. I applied for a grant for a particular family and was successful and the family went away for a week safe in the knowledge that the holiday destination catered for children with disabilities. Go to https://www.familyfund.org.uk for more information.

## Holiday play scheme

When I moved to North Wales from South Wales in 2009, I found to my disappointment that the schools in the local authority did not open during the summer and Easter holidays to offer play support. Parents could apply for their children to have 6 days of 'play' during the summer holidays, and this meant that they would access a designated facility for those 6 days and that was it.

As our students' homes are spread out across the authority it is difficult for them to meet up during the holidays. I had been an assistant head of a special school in Cheltenham that opened throughout the summer for our students to have the opportunity to meet up and play together. A HLTA at the school ran the holiday play scheme and the parents association raised the funds to ensure its continuance.

I was determined to replicate the scheme. I was very lucky to meet the local authority Out of Hours Learning Coordinator named Lesley Courtney who agreed with me that it was needed. She was also determined to find the funds so that we could open for a week in the Easter holidays and for five of the six-week summer holidays. Our school opened in September 2009 and ran its first holiday play scheme in the Easter of 2010. Lesley got the funding and sorted out the staff payroll and training for the first couple of years. Once the funding was no longer available, Lesley put us in touch with Clybiau Plant Cymru. They would support us in applying for funding and our parents' association took over Lesley's role. If any school or parent's association wishes to have a holiday play scheme running, you are based in Wales, and need support to set it up then Clybiau Plant Cymru should be your first contact. For more information go to Home | Clybiau Plant Cymru Kids' Clubs. Lottery funding has kept our play scheme running ever since but Jo Smith, from Clybiau Plant Cymru, took our parents association through the funding application process.

We were very lucky that our staff wanted to work during the holidays and Lesley, and I made sure that the pay and conditions met with staff approval. The club ran four days a week in the first year from the hours of 10.00am to 2.00pm. This was increased from 10.00am to 3.00pm for subsequent years. HLTAs and teaching assistants trained in club management and ran the holiday clubs. They shared the responsibility so that no member of staff worked the full 5 weeks of the holiday period unless they chose to. It was staffed entirely by people who also worked for the school. This ensured a very highly skilled and experienced team who also knew all the children attending well. The club was able to use bases in the school and all the playground facilities so that the children were happy and confident in their surroundings.

The club limited its spaces to 16 children a day, aged between 3 and 11 years, with 8 members of staff and the club's manager in the first year. This was subsequently increased to 30 children with appropriate staffing levels. Each child was assigned a key worker who was responsible for them each day.

Essential training had to be put in place for those who had not worked with students with specific needs. This was to ensure the worker had the correct skills and knowledge to provide the level of support needed. This included training in personal care and feeding as well as training linked to medication for conditions such as epilepsy and diabetes. Communication passports and specialist equipment were also essential. So too were policies and information packs which would include details of the rooms that I, as the headteacher, with the support of the governing body, allowed the club to use. Photos of workers and a timetable of activities were provided as this allowed parents to prepare their child for the experience.

It can sometimes be difficult for our students to be accepted by ordinary children at local playgrounds. I remember a parent coming to see me when we opened the holiday play scheme for the first time. Her son had been assaulted twice at the park opposite her house by two boys of similar age to her son. He had tried to make friends with them but because he was different, they first teased him and then assaulted him. She spoke to the boy's parents, but her son refused to go to the park again. She was grateful that he had the play scheme to attend.

An added bonus was that our students who attended the play scheme had less transition problems when returning to school in the autumn term as they had not had that 6-week break. We wanted the play provision to foster children's independence and self-esteem and encourage them to develop basic play skills. We provided feeding and medication by experienced staff. Daily routines were maintained, and specialist equipment and facilities were available. Policies for you to copy or adapt are available in the resource chapter.

Some authorities run their own play clubs and offer therapeutic play sessions, half term and summer play schemes. Torfaen play and short breaks service support over 200 children and young people across the borough with learning disabilities including complex medical needs and profound disabilities to attend play sessions. If you wish to find out more about how Torfaen manage to provide this visit http://torfaen.gov.uk

# Breakfast play club

It was also important when we opened to provide a breakfast play club for our students. It would give parents respite and provide students with play opportunities before school began. It would ensure that all students had breakfast. We would work on the healthy bit. Many of our students had sensory issues regarding food.

We were very fortunate that the Welsh government funded the club and the salaries of staff. Breakfast club staff had job descriptions (see the Resource chapter if you wish to copy them) and we monitored and evaluated its effectiveness regularly and this provided evidence to the local authority for its continued need. Staff serving breakfast trained in basic food hygiene and safety.

Parents were very glad of the breakfast club, and I remember Rhodri Morgan, the first minister for Wales, visiting the school in 2009. He was thrilled that we had two-third of our students taking up the opportunity to attend breakfast club. Some parents were able to take on employment for the first time. Our breakfast club gave them qualified childcare for their children who often had severe healthcare needs.

There is no legal requirement on a governing body to provide free breakfasts and schools that do not take part in the Welsh Government Scheme can run their own and charge parents. Certainly, some schools in North Wales provide free breakfast but charge for extra childcare outside of the half-hour expected to eat breakfast.

I would disagree with the half-hour time allowance for special schools as many of our students need support to eat their breakfast. I would gauge an hour as a more reasonable time allowance to ensure all students are catered for. In fact, our breakfast club opened at 8.30 and finished at 9.30 when school started. When I left the school in 2019, we were still being funded for the hour by the local authority, who were in turn funded by the Welsh Government, to provide healthy breakfasts to our students and to supervise the students.

Play facilities for the breakfast club were also funded and our manager of the breakfast club, one of our HLTAs met with the senior leadership team regularly to update us on the needs of the students and revisit the action plan that was a part of our SIP.

I monitored the club regularly and was pleased to see excellent supervision of students eating breakfast or being fed breakfast. Others might be playing with indoor games, toys and construction sets or, weather permitting, outside on the playgrounds. Individuals with a sensory processing issue might be using a sensory room to learn to self-regulate.

If you do not have access to a free breakfast club then Kellogg's Breakfast club network is a network that gives grants to schools to set up breakfast clubs in the UK. Email them to find out more breakfastclubUK@kellogg.com

## After school play provision

It is a concern that once the school day is over for children in a special school, they might live an isolated life at home. There are some clubs available to them and a very successful one in the Flintshire area, where my school was based was a club known as D.A.F.F.O.D.I.L.S. I visited the club to see what they offered our students. It was open one evening a week, but it also provided days out for its club members. It was all about play.

I have observed some excellent after school provision in mainstream schools where full use is made of all the play facilities and the supervision matches the needs of the students. I have also observed good after school provision in secondary special schools, but I have not seen many primary special schools provide this facility. It could be because it is difficult for parents to collect their children from the provision and there is also a charge for After School Club. It is not free. In the 10 years that I was head of a primary special school, we regularly offered parents the opportunity for this but apart from a six-month stint at providing drama club parents did not take us up on the offer.

In the next and final chapter of this book, there are many resources that you may choose to copy or adapt for use in your own organisation.

# Resources

Magic therapy policy
Sun protection policy
Lesson plan on use of bikes
Forest school policy
Outdoor play policy
Climbing wall policy
MDS Job description
Job description
Lunchtime policy
Sensory profile
Individual Education Plan (IEP)
DIR floor time intervention report
DIR floortime™ policy
Impact report on play therapy
Soft play rules
Venture into play policy
Breakfast club assistant
Holiday play scheme resources

DOI: 10.4324/9781003206538-11

# RESOURCE: Magic therapy policy

This policy explains the nature of Magic Therapy Hocus Focus™ Wizard's Club within the school and its contribution to the education of students at our school.

This policy has been shared and approved by the teaching staff and school governors.

## Aims

Magic Therapy offers students the opportunity to:

- Develop their gross and fine motor skills
- Increase their self-efficacy, self-esteem, group interaction and interpersonal skills
- Increase their attention and perception
- Develop their motor planning skills
- Develop their cognitive skills

Magic Therapy should be a personal and pleasurable experience, which enriches the lives of the students and those around them.

## What is magic therapy?

Healing of magic is a carefully designed, systematic approach to the therapeutic use of simple magic tricks in physical and psychosocial rehabilitation. It has been utilised in many areas:

**Physical Diagnoses** – For all physical diagnoses, it is effective in increasing the client's ability to manipulate objects (dexterity, grasp and release) as well as gross motor skills.

**Brain Injury** – Performing magic tricks provides cognitive and perceptual challenges for clients with acquired brain injury.

**Spinal Injury** – For the spinal cord injured client with limited hand function, it allows for mastery of their environment without requiring skilful hand movements.

**Mental Health** – In areas of mental health, magic has been utilised to augment processes. It is effective in increasing frustration tolerance, task-follow through, concentration, group co-operation, impulse control, communication and many other goals.

**Education** – For students who face additional challenges – learning disabilities, emotional behaviour disorders, developmental and cognitive delays and autism – learning magic may have a significant impact on neurodevelopmental function, i.e., attention, memory, language, temporal-sequential ordering, spatial ordering, neuromotor functions, social cognition and higher-order cognition.

## Introduction

The art of illusion has captivated people for thousands of years. It is perhaps the oldest of all the performing arts. References of magicians performing in the Courts of the Pharaohs date back as far as 5000 B.C. Magic has a long and rich history.

Award-winning illusionist Kevin Spencer set up the Foundation of the Healing of Magic. His work is focussed on researching arts-integrated interventions for clients and providing relevant, useful and engaging continuing education for therapists. For additional information, please visit www.magictherapy.com and www.HocusFocusEducation.com

## Entitlement

We endorse the aims of the National Curriculum to provide a broad and balanced curriculum and deliver magic therapy to enable students to improve cognition, motor skills, communication and social skills so that they may better access the curriculum.

## Planning

The Wizard's Club leader follows the Hocus Focus Curriculum designed by Kevin Spencer. Teachers match educational targets, where possible from the school assessment tool. They share and discuss those targets with the Wizard's Club leader. The Wizard's Club leader and the teacher may also choose targets that support the well-being of the student. Teachers set different targets to meet the specific needs of individual students.

## Equal opportunities

Magic Therapy is delivered to students regardless of gender, culture or ability. Boys and girls have equal access to this therapy.

## Resources

Magic Therapy is delivered in a multipurpose room at the school by a Wizard's Club leader. During the beginning of each session students greet each other, go through the Wizard's Academy Code of Ethics, and recite the Wizard's Promise. Students have 10 magic tricks to learn throughout the course. Students learn these tricks using the Hocus Focus DVD and visual step by step guides provided. Students have the opportunity to practice and perform each trick during the session. During some sessions, students will be given Wizard's Castle homework tasks, which involves students learning and performing tricks at home for family and friends. At the end of each session, students reflect on the session using their Wizard's Book of Secrets and Wizard's Academy Chart. Students are also awarded a welcome certificate after their first session and a diploma certificate for completing the 10 magic tricks at the end of the course.

A table with chairs around is used for the delivery of Wizard's Club. Students learn the magic trick around the table and are given the opportunity to perform their magic trick on the 'stage'. A relaxed and minimal distraction-free environment is maintained. A laptop and the Hocus Focus DVD are used to present the magic trick and follow the step-by-step instructions. An object of reference/signifier is also used (a small magic wand) to aid the understanding of students. Students are prepared for Magic Therapy by a social story and the Magic Therapy is referred to Wizard's Club by all staff for the students.

## Assessment, recording and reporting of student progress

The evaluation of learning outcomes comes from individual assessment planning and this eva-luation is used to inform future planning. The Wizard's Club leader records the progress made by students towards their targets after each session and also records any evidence that the therapy has supported the well-being of the student. This recording sheet is copied and placed in an individual Wizard's Club class file. The teacher uses this evidence to write end of session reports home to inform parents of the progress made by their child and also writes reports for each student's annual review.

An evaluation sheet is completed by the class teacher to show the impact of the therapy on the students learning and/or health.

## Monitoring and evaluation of magic therapy

The therapies consultant carries out detailed monitoring and evaluation of Magic Therapy. As part of the process, the consultant looks at all aspects of how Magic Therapy is delivered in school and its relationship to student progress. An action plan for further development is then drawn up. Monitoring and evaluation are carried out on a rolling programme every two years.

## Supervision

The Wizard's Club leader has overall responsibility for the supervision and general safety of all those receiving a therapeutic session of Magic Therapy.

The Wizard's Club leader will evaluate every application to assess the student's suitability to receive Magic Therapy.

## Data handling

It is essential that the Wizard's Club leader maintains appropriate and detailed records. They must ensure they are kept confidentially and adhere to data protection legislation ensuring all records held are appropriate and stored securely.

## Health and hygiene

The Wizard's Club leader must ensure they maintain a safe environment for their clients. The Wizard's Club room should be warm, clean and comfortable and be free from all potential hazards.

## Risk assessments

A risk assessment should be carried out in respect of each student referred for Wizard's Club. This will include any mobility issues that may require the use of the hoist and an individual manual handling plan will be put in place if necessary. If a student has a medical condition that requires constant monitoring it may be deemed necessary for an additional member of staff to accompany the student to ensure their individual health needs are being met.

## Accident procedures

All accidents or incidents that occur whilst in the Wizard's Club room or on the way to or from the Wizard's Club room must be immediately reported to the Head Teacher and guidance sought from a qualified first aider if appropriate. An accident form should be obtained from the school office and completed timeously (within 24 hours of the incident/accident).

## Other guidance

It is appreciated that whilst every care may be taken to promote safety, they may be occasions and situations that occur despite safety precautions being in place. In such an eventuality further clarification and advice will be sought from the Head Teacher who may seek further guidance from the local authority.

As a Rights Respecting School we are committed to embedding the principles and values of the United Nations Convention for the Rights of the Child (UNCRC). This policy ensures that our students have access to and are supported in the following articles of the convention.

| Article 1 | Every child under the age of 18 has all the rights in the Convention |
| Article 29 | Education must develop every child's personality, talents and abilities to the full |
| Article 31 | Every child has the right to relax, play and take part in a wide range of cultural and artistic activities |
| Article 42 | Every child has the right to know their rights |

# RESOURCE: Sun protection policy

This policy was reviewed through the process of consultation with Health and Safety person and teaching/non-teaching staff and parents.

At our school, we acknowledge the importance of sun protection and want staff and students to enjoy the sun safely. We will work with staff, pupils and parents to achieve this.

Too much exposure to ultraviolet light (UV) radiation from the sun causes sunburn, skin damage and increases the risk of skin cancer. Sun exposure in the first 15 years of life contributes significantly to the lifetime risk of skin cancer. There is enormous potential for schools to help prevent skin cancer in future generations. Schools are central to protecting children's skin this is because:

- Children are at school five out of seven days a week at times when UV rays are high.
- Most damage due to sun exposure occurs during the school years.
- Schools can play a significant role in changing behaviours through role modelling and education.
- Students and teachers are at risk of sunburn within 10–15 minutes of being exposed to strong sunlight.
- Students spend an average of 1.5 hours outside per school day, more if involved in sports and outdoor activities.
- Skin cancer is largely preventable through behaviour modification and sun protection during the early years.

## Education

These measures are in place from now:

- Parents and guardians will be sent letters explaining what the school is doing about sun protection and hope they can help at the beginning of the school year.
- Encourage parents to support the school by acting as role models and providing protection for their children.
- Be positive in your approach. Allow sun protection strategies to be fun, involve everyone, and provide choices.

## Protection

- This is an ongoing process.

## Shade

- We will encourage students to sit/play in the shade where it is possible and available.

## Timetabling

- We will aim to schedule outside side activities before 11am and after 3pm. Where this is unavoidable, we will ensure hats, clothing and sunscreen are worn to prevent sunburn.

## Clothing

- Children are encouraged to wear hats during outside activities, Hats are available for purchase as part of school uniform.

## Sunscreen

- We will send letters home asking for permission for staff to supervise children applying sunscreen.
- Staff will help children that are not able to apply sunscreen themselves only with parental consent.
- The letter will also ask for children to bring in their own sunscreen clearly labelled nothing less than SPF30.
- We cannot currently supply sunscreen to all children daily because of cost. We will supply sunscreen for children who forgot to bring it with them but only with parents' consent.

## Monitoring and review

- The governing body monitors our sun policy on an annual basis. Any findings and recommendations will be reported, and the policy will be modified, if necessary, the governing body gives serious consideration to any comments from parents about sun-protection policy and makes record of all such comments.

---------------------------------------------------------------------------------------------------

# RESOURCE: Lesson plan on use of bikes

## Cycling - Summer 2nd Half Term

| Week | Objective | Activity | B Squared Assessment | Resources |
|------|-----------|----------|----------------------|-----------|
| 1 | • Using bicycle riding equipment appropriately | Safety talk for specialist bicycles<br>Introduce equipment - helmets and bicycles and safe zone to cycle in<br>Pupils using bicycles according to ability<br>Staff supporting use of bicycles | P5 - Follow simple instructions with support<br>P6 - Waits patiently for a turn | Specialist bicycles<br>Cones/signs |
| 2 | • Getting on and off bicycle independently<br>• To practice stopping and starting | Safety talk and checking helmets<br>Guide pupils to bicycles and encourage to get on to bicycle independently where appropriate<br>Pupils and support practice cycling around circuit | P5 - Stops and starts under control<br>P6 - Movement: to stop | Specialist bicycles<br>Cones/signs |
| 3 | • To apply brakes appropriately<br>• To keep both feet on pedals whilst in motion where appropriate | Explain where brakes and pedals are<br>Practice starting and stopping exercise<br>Pupils practice using circuit with differentiated levels of support<br>Reinforce vocabulary brake, stop and pedal | P5 - To repeat activity to refine skill<br>P6 - To move freely and confidently | Specialist bicycles<br>Cones/signs |
| 4 | • To rehearse pedalling<br>• To reinforce use of the ball of the fool for pedalling | Revise previous session vocabulary and parts of bicycle<br>Demonstrate part of foot used for pedalling<br>Adults supporting pupils to practice this<br>Pupils pedalling around course using ball of foot for pedalling actions | P5 - To repeat activity to refine skill<br>P6 - To adjust technique to task and sequence movements to control bike | Specialist bicycles<br>Cones/signs |
| 5 | • To look/focus ahead whilst cycling | Revise vocabulary and actions so far<br>When pupils concentrate on their feet/bike, encourage them to look ahead to concentrate on obstacles/direction that they are wishing to travel | P5 - To be aware of the gradient of the ground whilst cycling<br>P6 - With support link movements learnt in sequence | Specialist bicycles<br>Cones/signs |
| 6 | • To stop independently using brakes | Rehearse concentrating on the course and looking ahead.<br>Demonstrate braking and practice stopping independently - use a stop sign where necessary to support pupils indicating where to stop<br>Practice cycling around the course | P6 Movement: to stop<br>P6 To continue to move freely using skills so far | Specialist bicycles<br>Cones/signs |

Notes: up to bikeability Level 1 module 4 notes

### Resource Forest School Long Term Plan

| Week | Autumn | Spring | Summer |
|------|--------|--------|--------|
| 1 | Autumn Watch – developing signs of Autumn identification wheel | Spring watch – Identifying Signs of Spring, starting a weather chart | Summer book introduction – what have you spotted? Summer activity |
| 2 | Leaf Printing and Leaf Crowns | Planting Daffodil Bulbs/Leeks – Watch Me Grow – Gift Pots | Woodland windows and photography – making eco picture frames |
| 3 | Tea stain and Berry Treasure Maps, making a simple compass | Designing and making a nest for birds to nest in | Dandelion 'invisible ink' – sensory art and mark making activities (summer bk) |
| 4 | Fruit Collecting and making jam, blackberry fool etc | Scents of Spring – picking, crushing and smelling safe Spring petals etc | Blindfold exploring – guiding and feeling woodland textures |
| 5 | Bird Identification charts and Bird Feeders, Bird watching | Making flower rainbows using flowers fallen from trees and petals | Songs of the wood picnic – make and take picnic listening to natural sounds |
| 6 | Making and identification wheel for animals and plants | Making a 'Journey stick' showing feelings and experiences | Pond dipping and searching under rocks for signs of life |
| 7 | Acorn hunt – collecting/burying acorns Making an imaginative 'elf house' | Animal footprint detectives – Loggerheads walk looking for tracks in mud | Mother's day flower arrangement |
| **Half Term** | | | |
| 1 | Jurassic Park – Making a dinosaur garden and footprint investigating | Loggerheads Maths Trail – collecting items from clues | Minibeasts – investigation tally chart of minibeasts found and identified |
| 2 | Grass People & planting hyacinth bulbs for Christmas present planting | Animals in spring – visit Greenfield valley petting park and signs of wildlife search | Making minibeast housing to encourage ladybirds etc |
| 3 | Herb gardens – developing smell | St David's Day Daffodil Art/Making Leek Soup | Visit Rhydymwyn visitor centre for a minibeast hunt |
| 4 | Nature problem solving – leaf detective Making a kite for windy weather | Texture trail – how many textures can you collect | Butterfly hunt and identification keys Symmetrical art – making a butterfly |
| 5 | Winter Tree art – Loggerheads Making a Christmas | Ancient Tree Hunt Activity Tree silhouette art | Fortune teller walk – I see a…... Make an origami fortune teller |
| 6 | Pine Cones – Collect/Decorate Stick weaving activity | Twig identification key – collecting and matching twig types to key | The Ugly Bug Ball making invitations for a group barbecue at the eco centre |
| 7 | Christmas present treasure hunt Decorative Plant Pots for Christmas | Tree faces – making 'faces' for trees as part of eco art (do NOT damage tree) | Barbecue and eco friendly party – twig crowns and eco art activities |

| Directorate | | | Activity (Brief Description) | Forest School | |
|---|---|---|---|---|---|
| Service | Education | | People at Risk | Students and Staff | |
| Location | A | | Date | | Review Date |
| | | | | | ongoing |
| Assessor | | | Issue Number | 1 | |
| Item No | Hazard (Include Defects) | RISK RATING (Without controls) High/Medium/Low | Existing Control Measures | | RISK RATING (With existing controls) High/Medium/Low |
| | Exploring the site. Uneven ground. Branches and tree roots on the ground, Branches, and shrubs at eye level. | Medium | Students well supervised. Awareness talks and reminders. There will always be at least 2 members of staff first aid trained, with the kit and mobile phone. Site checked regularly to ensure no falling or low-level branches. Cuts, small injuries were dealt on site. Serious injuries dealt with in school or using 999. Children are taught to be self-aware. | | Low |
| | Missing Child. A child may wander off or go missing during a Forest School session. | Low | Children were told and asked to repeat boundaries and Forest School Rules. Regular headcount. No access out of Forest School grounds. Children to realise the importance of following rules and working as a group. | | Low |
| | Bites and stings from bees, wasps, and stinging nettles | Low | Warn not to catch bees/wasps and to be aware of stinging nettles. Long trousers and closed footwear to be worn. Nettles to be cleared. | | Low |
| | Allergies or children's existing conditions | Low | | | |

| Hazard | Risk | Control measures | Residual risk |
|---|---|---|---|
| Mushrooms and poisonous plants | Low | Opportunity to study insects rather than being frightened of them. | Low |
| Building dens, using sticks and branches | Low | All staff to be aware of any known allergies or existing conditions and treatment required. Promote knowledge and independence in identifying and avoiding allergens. | |
| Animal droppings | Low | Ensure children do not eat anything they find, keep their hands out of their mouths and wash them thoroughly at the end of the session. | |
| Small tools: potato peelers, knives, saws, | High | Obvious mushrooms, poisonous plants to be cleared away. Promote identification of poisonous plants. | Low |
| Large tools: Sheaf knife, loppers, bow saw, bill hook | High | Children to be made aware of dangers and shown how to carry sticks carefully and be aware of others around them. | |
| Fire lighting and campfire | High | Children to be made aware and instructed not to pick up. Help children identify animals from their droppings by sight alone. | Low |
| Cooking food | High | Safety talk given and repeated regularly. Close supervision. | |
| Ingestion of toxins or poisons from flora and fauna. Zoonosis – Toxoplasmosis and Weil's disease. | Medium | Safety talk given and repeated regularly. Strict use on a 1–1 basis under very close supervision. Gloves to be used on the hand not holding tool. Only trained Forest leader allowed to use tools with children. | |
| Behavioural Issues | Medium | Safety talk given beforehand. Reminder of rules. | |

(Continued)

Only trained leader allowed to do fire lighting. Children only allowed in the fire circle when asked by trained leader on a 1–1 basis. Water always available by side of fire. Gloves used when needed. Children to sit on logs/planks while fire is lit. School to be informed when Forest school involves a fire.

Any food cooked will be under close supervision with the adult cooking the food and ensuring it is cooled before children eat it.

All staff delivering training courses will hold a relevant emergency first aid qualification, appropriate to the training being led, and carry a first aid kit.

Individual risk assessments completed before any student allowed to take part so as not to put others at risk.

*(Continued)*

| Item No | Further Action necessary to control risk | Action By | Date Completed | RESIDUAL RISK (With further controls) High/Medium/Low |
|---|---|---|---|---|
| **Assessor(s) Signature(s)** | Managers Name | | **Manager Signature** | |
| **Other relevant Risk Assessments:** | | | | |
| | No inexperienced staff allowed to take part. | Low | | |
| | | Medium | | |
| | *Ultimate Risk* | *HIGH* | *Ultimate Existing Risk* | *LOW* |

99

# RESOURCE: Forest school policy

## Aims

- Our school aims to use the natural environment to instil the Forest School values. This approach to outdoor play encourages students to develop independence, motivation, co-operative working with peers and adults, appropriate risk taking and an appreciation of the outdoor environment.
- Forest School builds on students development of play, interests and skills.
- Forest school leaders hope to develop students independence, self-esteem and communication skills as well as establishing positive relationships with others.
- Forest School explores the outdoors and the natural environment with practical, useful activities all year round.
- Forest School sessions are part of the children's learning experiences and part of the school week.
- Forest School has environmental awareness at its core.
- Wherever possible environmentally friendly products and recycled materials will be used.
- Staff will model good practice regarding care for the environment and all litter will be removed at the end of each session.
- The school grounds and any other outdoor areas used will be maintained to ensure the survival of all native flora and fauna and new flora will be introduced if needed.
- Brambles and nettles will be removed from the main pathways but apart from this will be allowed to grow. Likewise, branches at eye level will also be removed from main pathways to ensure safety. Our school will ensure minimal damage is done to the sites we use and their surrounding areas.
- If there are endangered plants these will be highlighted beforehand and a session on how we look after these species so that students feel empowered to protect the natural world without the fear of getting into trouble for picking a weed.

## Health and safety

Forest School aims to support students in developing appropriate risk-taking skills in a structured and controlled way. A high staffing ratio is always in place to ensure safety. For a Forest School session to take place, there must always be at least one trained Forest School leader in the session. A comprehensive risk assessment is in place which covers all possible activities and eventualities. Before each session, a risk assessment is carried out to assess risks such as weather or harmful plants on site. All students will wear appropriate clothing and footwear to Forest School dependent on the weather. Students are to wear long trousers when attending Forest School. Waterproof trousers and coats are available for all students to wear and are encouraged, particularly when the weather is cooler. If a fire is lit during a session, then a competent person is to stay with the fire. There will always be at least 10 litres of water available for putting out the fire and the fire should not be near low overhanging trees. The size of the fire will be dependent on the students involved and their previous behaviour around fires. Students will be supported to understand the rules around the fire. The school has a Health and Safety Policy and Safeguarding Policy to enhance aspects of health and safety.

## First Aid

The Forest School Leader has an enhanced first-aid certificate to specifically cover the outdoors. There will be a first aid kit taken into the designated area and extra first aid equipment is located within the school if required.

## Equality

Forest School is inclusive by nature. All students are included with all activities and no form of discrimination will take place; reasonable adjustments will be made to make it inclusive for all.

## Tools

Students will be taught how to use tools safely and correctly. When working with tools children will be working at a maximum ratio of 1 adult to 2 children. The use of tools will be covered in the risk assessment. Using tools with students should be carried out on a 1:1 basis to begin with. Students should be introduced to tools gradually with tool use beginning with a potato peeler. As their experience within Forest School progresses this can be extended. Tools should be put away clean. All tools should be returned to the box or bag when not in use. The tool should not be left unattended.

## Staffing

The Forest School Leader will have a Forest School Leader qualification, DBS enhanced disclosure and an outdoor first aid qualification. The Forest School Leader will have the overall responsibility for:

- Risk assessments, pre-visit site checks and continuous safety monitoring.
- Planning for sessions including differentiation for individual children's needs.
- Ensuring necessary equipment is taken into woodland.
- Administration of first aid and first aid kit.
- Supervision of tools use, cleaning and storing.
- Organising emergency procedures.

## Staff and volunteers will

- model good practice throughout the session
- carry out delegated roles and responsibilities
- extend children's learning where appropriate
- support children to manage their own risk
- remind children of rules and boundaries
- be aware of dangers within Forest School
- monitor levels of safety at all times
- support the Forest School leader to run the sessions

## Emergency procedures

The Forest School Leader will be responsible for phoning the emergency services if required. All staff will be aware of emergency procedures and reminded regularly.

The Leader will have a mobile phone during sessions and the necessary information for the emergency services as well as leaving a copy with the school office on leaving the school building. After an accident or emergency, it is imperative that staff complete the necessary records.

## Cancellations

There may be times when Forest School sessions have to be cancelled due to unforeseen circumstances.

These may be:

- Staff illness – which prevents staff/child ratios from being met.
- Severe weather conditions.
- Any situation that poses a health and safety risk.

As a Rights Respecting School we are committed to embedding the principles and values of the United Nations Convention for the Rights of the Child (UNCRC). This policy ensures that our students have access to and are supported in the following articles of the convention.

Article 1 Every child under the age of 18 has all the rights in the Convention

Article 29 Education must develop every child's personality, talents and abilities to the full

Article 31 Every child has the right to relax, play and take part in a wide range of cultural and artistic activities

# RESOURCE: Outdoor play policy

It is important that students should be given the opportunity, on a regular basis, to enjoy energetic activity both indoors and out and the feeling of well-being that it brings. Outdoor play provides an environment that responds to individual learning styles. It complements and enhances all aspects of students' development and learning through its physical and open-ended nature

## *Aims*

- We aim to provide a safe and secure, yet stimulating environment for all students to explore, engage and learn in the outdoor area.
- We aim to provide experiences that will enable all students to progress in all aspects of skills and areas of learning through the vehicle of play.
- We aim to ensure that all staff understand the value of outdoor play and so are enthusiastic and active in their approach to learning outside

## *Entitlement*

- All students will be given the opportunity to access the outdoor area during continuous provision planning sessions, moving freely between indoors and outdoors
- The resources provided will support learning across the curriculum
- As indoors we will identify continuous provision for outdoors (see separate sheet)
- Planning will reflect individual interests, develop group work and thematic play
- The "Show me 5 Rules" (these rules are taken from the Behaviour programme that can be found at http://incredibleyears.com) will be promoted in the outdoor area to promote a safe and secure environment
- Practitioners will have regard for health and safety whilst allowing opportunity for positive risk taking
- Practitioners will act as positive role models and facilitators of students' learning
- Equality of play opportunities will be promoted by all adults supporting outdoor sessions

## *Content*

The topics and skills for the Foundation Phase are based on the Foundation Phase curriculum and focus on exploring their immediate environment for students within Year 2 are also based on the Foundation Phase and enhanced by using an adapted National Curriculum. The schemes of work are adapted to meet the needs of students with MLD: SLD and PMLD.

In the Foundation Phase, outdoor play focuses on understanding the world around us and embracing the outdoors to develop a range of skills.

## Planning

We use a skills-based approach to planning within the Foundation Phase and it is very much a child-led approach in which the topics are led from the interest of the students.

Outdoor continuous provision, enhanced provision, topic-based medium-term plans and outdoor challenges are produced termly, with input from all department teachers to ensure that there is progression and continuity of content.

Staff may work with the whole task using directed tasks or support small groups in their learning and play.

## Equal opportunities

We are committed to equalising opportunities for all students to succeed, irrespective of gender, culture or ability. Outdoor play will help to develop the pupils' awareness of the world around, and will make use of the pupils' own experiences, challenging stereotypes, promoting positive images and presenting a view of alternative ways of living.

## Special needs

All teachers must make themselves aware of any relevant medical problem or particular learning difficulty, which may affect a pupils' ability to learn.

The planning for the topics and directed activities give suggestions for possible methods of delivery. These can be adapted to suit particular students by referring to the PMLD and Alternative Curriculum materials.

## ICT

There is opportunity to use ICT within the outdoor areas such as through cameras, video cameras, remote control vehicles and 'walkie talkies'.

## Resources

A range of resources for outdoor play are available and are kept in storage within the different outdoor areas, blue class, red and orange and yellow and green.

## Assessment, recording and reporting of student progress

Teachers write weekly plans which may use the outdoor environment as an extension of the classroom provision. Annual targets and IEP's may also be assessed within the outdoors where applicable. Ongoing observations, annotated photo sheets and photographs are used to record and assess which form the part of each individual students 'learning journey'. Floor books record the class's topic books and scrapbooks record whole-class work during continuous provision planning. Both the child's learning journeys and assessments are evaluated termly and facilitate planning for the next unit. Parents are informed of work covered and progress made in the pupils' Annual Report, home–school diaries and regular correspondence.

## Monitoring and evaluation

The Head Teacher carries out detailed monitoring and evaluation of the foundation phase in- cluding outdoor provision and play. The Head Teacher looks at all aspects of how it is delivered and its relationship to student progress. An action plan for further development is then drawn up. Monitoring and evaluation are carried out regularly.

## Health and safety

Due the nature of outdoor play, the safety of students must be paramount, and health and safety guidelines rigorously adhered to. Risk assessments have also been completed and reviewed for all outdoor areas within the department.

## Review

This policy will be reviewed in the light of any changes in the Early Learning Goals or the National Curriculum.

As a Rights Respecting School we are committed to embedding the principles and values of the United Nations Convention for the Rights of the Child (UNCRC). This policy ensures that our students have access to and are supported in the following articles of the convention.

Article 1 Every child under the age of 18 has all the rights in the Convention

Article 29 Education must develop every child's personality, talents and abilities to the full

Article 31 Every child has the right to relax, play and take part in a wide range of cultural and artistic activities

# RESOURCE: Climbing wall policy

Procedure for admission of a student to climbing activities:

- A qualified school instructor assesses the suitability of the student for climbing activity and, if necessary, conducts a risk assessment and identifies safety measures.
- The instructor informs the student about rules and safety measures.

Procedure for a support assistant to oversee climbing activities:

- The support assistant is informed about Climbing Wall Rules and Procedures.
- The support assistant signs the Climbing Wall User Statement.

School Climbing-Instructor Assistant (for indoor high climbing wall):

- Inspects equipment and climbing wall prior to every bouldering session.
- Collects the key and signs a logbook.
- Ensures the number of assistants is sufficient for the climbing session (minimal ratio 1:2).
- Assesses readiness of students and assistants for climbing activity.
- Organises the activity regarding the pupil's specific needs and abilities and conducts a risk assessment prior to the session if necessary.
- Checks correct fitting and use helmets.
- Inspects equipment after the session and reports to the Climbing Instructor immediately any fault or loose/damaged hold on the wall.
   Reports any accident/incident during the session to the Climbing Instructor.
- Suspends any student or support assistant from climbing activity who disregards rules and procedures or compromises safety and gives a written report to the Climbing Instructor.

Climbing Instructor (for indoor high climbing wall):

- Inspects equipment and climbing wall prior to every session.
- Collects the key and signs a logbook.
- Ensures the number of co-workers is sufficient for the climbing session (minimal ratio 1:2).
- Assesses readiness of students and co-workers for climbing activity.
- Organises the activity regarding the pupil's specific needs and abilities and conducts a risk assessment prior to the session if necessary.
- Checks the attachment of climbers to the rope and harness before every climb as well as correct fitting and use of device.
- Inspects equipment after the session and reports to the Senior Management immediately any fault or loose/damaged hold on the wall.
- Reports any accident/incident during the session to the Senior Management and completes the necessary documents.

Suspends any student or support assistant from climbing activity who disregards rules and procedures or compromises safety and gives a written report to the Senior Management by the end of the day.

A member of the Senior Management Team:

- Organises an assessment of climbing instructors by the external agency and keeps the list of school instructors up to date.
- Reviews the skills of school instructors at a minimum six-monthly interval if this is delegated by an external Advisor.
- Ensures that all school instructors are familiar with these Rules and Procedures and General Risk Assessment for Climbing Activity.
- Maintains wall and equipment.
- Acts on any reported accident/incident and gives a written report to the Governing body.
- Suspends any student or support assistant from any climbing wall activity who disregards rules and procedures or compromises safety.

Rules for Indoor high Climbing Wall:

- Only a qualified school climbing instructor or co-instructor may collect the key and equipment and sign the logbook.
- Use of the climbing wall by students unaccompanied and unsupervised by a School Instructor is forbidden.
- All equipment must be inspected before and after each session, and any faults reported immediately to the Senior management.
- Any loose or damaged holds on the wall must either be tightened/replaced or removed from the wall and reported to the Climbing Instructor and the Senior management.
- Only two students/co-workers may climb at the same time on each wall.
- Climbers and belayers must wear helmets during the activity and no rings, jewellery or overly lose clothing, long hair must be tied back.
- When not bouldering, climbing may only take place when the climber is attached to the rope using a recognised method, checked by the Climbing Instructor.
- The space directly around the wall must be always kept clear.
- Students may only belay each other at the discretion of the Climbing Instructor, and only with the second belayer to assist with rope management.
- When bouldering, each pupil/support assistant must not have their feet higher than 1 metre (blue and black holds) from the floor and be "spotted" by a suitable individual.
- Students may only "spot" each other at the discretion of the Climbing Instructor and only when a support assistant is in proximity.
- All equipment and the key must be returned after each session by the Climbing Instructor.

| Directorate | | Activity (Brief Description) | Climbing Wall | |
|---|---|---|---|---|
| Service | | People at Risk | Students and Staff | |
| Location | | Date | | Review Date: ongoing |
| Assessor | | Issue Number | 1 | |

| Item No | Hazard (Include Defects) | RISK RATING (Without controls) High/Medium/Low | Existing Control Measures | RISK RATING (With existing controls) High/Medium/Low |
|---|---|---|---|---|
| | Falling (causing head injury, serious tissue Injury or bruises) | Medium | Participants wear appropriate safety equipment. Close supervision at all times. Controlled environment | Low |
| | Structural failure of wall | Medium | Wall designed to BS-EN12572-1-2007. Regular maintenance of wall carried out by designated person with responsibility for sending regular report to governing body. | Low |
| | Misuse of Climbers safety equipment / detachment of rope from harness | High | Lessons given to students before use of climbing wall. Warnings given and visual reminders of the danger of readjusting equipment. Visual checks given by instructors consistently. Replace if necessary. | Low |
| | Falling objects | medium | No-one allowed to wear jewellery or carry items in pockets | Low |
| | Climbing onto the top of the wall | High | Lanyards attached to anyone posing a risk | Low |
| | Trip Hazard | Medium | Before session commences check area for any trip hazard and remove. Constant vigilance during session | Low |

| Hazard | Risk | Control Measures |
|---|---|---|
| **Strain on staff from handling students into position** | Medium | Ensure all staff have suitable manual handling training |
| **Wear and tear of Equipment leading to breakage** | Medium | Clean equipment after every session. Cancel session if equipment is not suitable for use |
| **Behavioural Issues Medical Issues** | High | Staff support throughout activities. Carefully selected instruments and equipment Staff trained in basic first aid. Room is nearby to .... classroom who is onsite in the event of summoning assistance. Risk Assessments of individual students carried out before beginning session if this is a known behaviour by pupil. StudentsIBP in individual folder and followed by staff. Staff aware of pupil's IBP. Clear boundaries set at start Staff trained in positive behaviour strategies and de-escalation techniques. Students care plans in place and followed by staff. Staff aware of pupil's medical needs and rescue meds taken to room. Staff trained in medical needs.Adequate staffing required if necessary Risk Assessments of individual students carried out before beginning therapy if necessary. Room is near ... classroom who is onsite in the event of summoning assistance. |

| | | | |
|---|---|---|---|
| Safeguarding | medium | Staff to follow safeguarding procedures of school and to have attended safeguarding training | low |
| | | Risk Assessments of individual students medical and /or behavioural needs carried out before beginning session if necessary | |
| Ultimate Risk | HIGH | Ultimate Existing Risk | LOW |

| Item No | Further Action necessary to control risk | Action By | Date Completed | RESIDUAL RISK (With further controls) High/Medium/Low |
|---|---|---|---|---|
| Assessor(s) Signature(s) | Managers Name | | Manager Signature | |
| Other relevant Risk Assessments: | | | | |

# RESOURCE: Job description

Midday Supervisor

Hrs.:

**PURPOSE OF POST:** Under the general direction of the headteacher, and the direct supervision of the Senior MDS ensure the safety, general welfare of pupils.

Lunchtime supervisors are employed for 90 minutes per day Monday to Friday so that they may assist classes to help with toileting, hand washing and supervising children to the dining hall.

**PRINCIPAL RESPONSIBILITIES:**

- Assist students in eating their meal and developing associated skills. Undertake personal care of students as directed
- Supervise and participate in play activities appropriate to the age and development of the pupils. Follow feeding, personal care or behavioural programmes specified for individual pupils.
- Maintain a safe and clean environment over the lunch period
- Ensure the welfare and safety of pupils, reporting any accident, illness or injury to the School Nurse, Head Teacher or classroom staff
- Arrive in time for their lunch duty to ensure adequate supervision.
- Notify the senior MDS and school office if absent from work.
- Ensure appropriate behaviour is maintained in line with the school's Behaviour Policy and build good relationships with students.
- Record incidents or relevant observations onto the class communication note. Pass to the SMDS at the end of lunch, so the class teacher can be informed.
- Report any serious incidents or concerns to the SMDS or a member of SMT straight away.
- Report safeguarding concerns to the designated officer in line with school policy.
- Remain on school premises for the duration of the duty.
- Conduct themselves safely and appropriately on the playground and in the lunch hall.
- Ensure student safety at all times and intervene, when necessary, in activities that are not safe.
- Listen to the students and promote positive play.
- Supervise areas of the playground as directed by the SMDS or the playground rota.
- Report to SMDS if scheduled duties are completed or if a query arises regarding your role or responsibility.
- Dining Hall Supervision Have high expectations of behaviour and promote a calm, positive environment.
- Support students feeding needs when directed (training given)
- Ensure the cleanliness of the dining room furniture at all times.
- Deal with accidents/incidents and ensure hazards from breakages/spillages/illness are dealt with immediately using the hazard warning signs in the first instance.
- Wipe tables and stack chairs at the end of the lunchtime.
- Report any breakages, unsafe equipment or unsafe areas to the SMDS.

- Monitor the use of the toilets.
- APPRAISAL AND TRAINING The appraisal process is completed in line with the Appraisal Process for Support Staff. Targets are set and reviewed accordingly. Training will take place on a term basis and address the needs of the school as well as the individual. Communication for MDS can be found in the staffroom on the notice board and housekeeping meetings are held half termly.

All support staff are part of a whole school team. They are required to support the values and ethos of the school and school priorities as defined in the School Improvement Plan. This will mean focussing on the needs of colleagues, parents and students and being flexible in a busy pressurised environment.

This job profile sets out the duties of the post at the time it was drawn up. The post holder may be required from time to time to undertake other duties within the school as may be reasonably expected, without changing the general character of the duties or level of responsibility entailed. This is a common occurrence and would not justify a reconsideration of the grading of the post. It will be reviewed regularly and may be subject to modification or amendment after consultation with the post holder.

# RESOURCE: Job description

Senior Midday Supervisor

Hrs. required:

**PURPOSE OF POST:** Under the general direction of the headteacher, direct and supervise the midday supervisory assistants, to ensure the safety, general welfare of the students during this period.

I

**PRINCIPAL RESPONSIBILITIES:**

- Direct, supervise and deploy midday supervisory assistants over the lunchtime period. Contribute to the recruitment, induction and appraisal of team members
- Resolve any operational issues and problems relating to midday supervision, involving the headteacher, as necessary.
- Supervise students during midday lunch break – including students who have a school meal as well as students who bring their own food.
- Supervise pupils' eating and feeding and assist where required
- Monitor lunchtime supervision to ensure students have a high-quality lunchtime experience and are kept safe at all times
- When children are sick or have accidents, come to their initial aid and summon qualified assistance where necessary.
- Supervise students in all areas of the school as required, always ensuring that students conduct themselves safely.
- Facilitate communication between the SMT and the MDS team.
- Advise the Headteacher and Deputy Headteacher on the effective deployment of the team
- Maintain an awareness of the staff development needs within the team and disseminate information about opportunities in this area.
- Keep notes of any meetings.
- Remain on school premises for the duration of your duty.
- Manage student behaviour under the guidance of the behaviour coordinator and with the support of the duty teacher, HLTA and build good relationships with students.
- Be aware of any extra-curricular activities or school visits that may impact on the lunchtime.
- Report any observations or concerns to the Duty teacher as they arise.
- Reporting safeguarding concerns to the designated officer in line with school policy.
- Cascade relevant information to MDS and respond to day to day queries as appropriate.
- Check weather conditions/safety of playground to decide if lunchtime play is indoors or outdoors and discuss with duty teacher/HLTA
- Organise cover for MDS staff absence when appropriate.
- Be aware of any extra-curricular activities or visits/visitors who may impact on the lunchtime.
- Co-ordinate activities and resources appropriately.
- Collate class communication notes at the end of lunch. Make a copy of the lunchtime file. Distribute to class teachers to follow up as appropriate.

- Organise relevant class lists for MDS on door duty – ensure absent students are marked off.
- In the absence of the SMDS, a member of SMT will arrange cover for MDS staff
- Appraisal and training The appraisal process is completed in line with the Appraisal Process for Support Staff. Targets are set and reviewed accordingly. Training will take place on a termly basis and address the needs of the school as well as the individual. Communication for MDS can be found in the staffroom on the notice board and housekeeping meetings are held half termly.

All support staff are part of a whole school team. They are required to support the values and ethos of the school and school priorities as defined in the School Improvement Plan. This will mean focussing on the needs of colleagues, parents and students and being flexible in a busy pressurised environment.

This job profile sets out the duties of the post at the time it was drawn up. The post holder may be required from time to time to undertake other duties within the school as may be reasonably expected, without changing the general character of the duties or level of responsibility entailed. This is a common occurrence and would not justify a reconsideration of the grading of the post. It will be reviewed regularly and may be subject to modification or amendment after consultation with the post holder.

**Signed**................................................................ **Date**..........................

# RESOURCE: Lunchtime policy

Every child has the right to enjoy a positive lunchtime experience. The experience should be positive, and students will be supported by a teacher on the playground, a HLTA in the dining hall, Teaching Assistants (TAs) and Mid-Day supervisors (MDSs). Senior teaching staff are always available and on duty during the lunch period. In our school, a teacher will supervise the playground at lunchtime on a voluntary basis and a rota system is in place. Teachers on duty can receive a free school dinner.

## Aims

To create an enjoyable and calm lunchtime environment

To promote the school PSHE and Healthy Schools programme and help students develop appropriate social skills through the attitude and behaviours of staff.

To ensure that all students feel safe and valued and that they.

Eat a healthy balanced lunch where possible

Have a break from structured routines and adult-led activities

Go to the toilet

Take exercise to improve health and fitness

Develop new skills, find new challenges and take risks

Develop friendships

Talk to staff members in more informal situations

Choose to be alone or part of a group

Take responsibility for own actions

Learn to play together

Students will be encouraged to play outside as much as possible.

## Organisation

The lunchtime rota will indicate when each MDS is on duty and the responsibility area. The rota will be reviewed each term and where possible responsibilities will vary. The rota will be distributed at the beginning of each term. In the absence of staff, the Senior MDS will adapt the rota and some MDS may be asked to cover in a different area.

## Specific lunchtime duties for all lunchtime staff include

- Responsibility for all students on school premises across the planned lunchtimes.
- Being punctual, ensuring adequate supervision at all times

- Students are served their meals until deemed to be independent enough to collect their own meals.
- Supervise children in the hall: collecting dinners, modelling the cutting of food, distributing drinks, etc.
- On exit the children should be encouraged to put their pack up boxes on the appropriate trolley and to put their coats on before lining up to leave the hall.
- At the end of the lunch period the teacher for each class arrives and asks the children to line up.
- Teachers relieve lunchtime supervisors and collect their class from the hall or playground (If for whatever reason the teacher does not appear on time, MDSs, should stay with the class until the teacher/TA arrives to collect them, however, this should only be in exceptional circumstances).
- Students should never be on the playground, in the dining room or in the classroom unsupervised.
- Manage behaviour in line with the school's Behaviour Policy.
- Report safeguarding concerns in line with school policy.
- Qualified first aiders administer emergency First Aid cover across the duty period.
- Notify duty teacher of the absence of MDS, TAs and students in line with staff absence policy, who will then notify the Senior Supervisor. (In the absence of the Duty teacher, notify the school office, who will notify the Senior Supervisor or an alternative member of the Senior Leadership Team.)
- All staff have the responsibility to ensure the health and safety of all students in their charge.
- All staff, including MDS staff, have job descriptions that are available for all to read. A copy may be requested from the school office (Please find copies in the Resource chapter of this book).

## *Practice*

Those students not in the Dining Hall will play on the Foundation/Key Stage 2 playgrounds or in a designated area of the school.

Dining hall procedures: Students in the Foundation Department and those students in KS2 having a hot meal or packed lunch will enter the Dining Hall in an order determined by department meetings and sanctioned by SMT.

Lunch hour is from 12 to 1pm. Currently the Foundation Dept use the dining hall from 12.00 to 12.30 and KS2 use the dining hall from 12.30 to 1pm.

When students are not in the hall they are out on the playground or in an indoor classroom reserved for students who are vulnerable and choose to stay indoors for lunch play.

This lunch rota alongside the timetable for indoor play will be posted on the notice board

People with autism can display hyper-sensitivity to food textures, heat and flavour. This can result in both a demand for especially bland foods or, in contrast, foods which, perhaps through crunchiness or saltiness, provide a sensory hit.

While a rigidity of diet – a pronounced liking for a very narrow range of foods – is quite common, the need to separate ingredients either on one plate means that we also have available the airplane tray systems that allow the cook and servers to isolate foods if necessary. All lunchtime staff need to bear this in mind.

Some parents have chosen a gluten- and casein-free diet as a "treatment" for autism. This needs to be considered.

All KS2 students having hot meals will eat in the Dining Hall when they are called from the relevant playground by the teacher in charge or the HLTA.

On entering the Dining Hall, the KS2 students having hot meals will collect them from the service hatch and join those having packed lunches at tables.

Use of ear defenders must be allowed for those students who cannot tolerate the noise of the lunch hall.

Students will leave the dining hall in class groups once their lunch session is over. iPads and other resources that class staff know are effective in keeping students occupied and engaged once they have eaten lunch may be brought in a box from class so that students do not disrupt others eating their lunch.

One named Supervisory Assistant will manage the use of bikes and all other members of lunchtime staff will organise outdoor play equipment. Equipment put out daily will be appropriate depending on the weather etc. KS2 has two playground areas, and these will be used according to need. If behaviours dictate the use of one playground for calm play with a high staff level may be required. This is reviewed regularly by the lunchtime team and SMT.

## Wet lunchtimes and playtimes

While the Head Teacher has overall responsibility for deciding whether it is indoor/outdoor play, the teacher on duty may decide upon the best course of action, depending on the playground conditions at the time. Students will only be kept indoors if it is unsafe to go outside or if the weather does not allow it. Students will be encouraged to take part in quiet settled activities during these sessions as space dictates. The lunchtime team have a wet games box room and a classroom dedicated to use of the White board for films that students may watch. This is so that students who wish to play games are not distracted by the film being shown. Students should remain in the designated 'Wet 'classes unless given a pass to Soft Play or another therapy room. Passes are determined by individual needs and sanctioned by SMT.

Basic First Aid will be administered from teaching assistants qualified and designated as first aiders. Relevant paperwork, where necessary should be completed once treatment has been administered and given to office staff to file. Parents should always be informed, preferably by a witness to the accident. Any incidents should be reported in the accident book with a description of the treatment given. The designated first aider will liaise with the school office regarding a phone call or letter home if appropriate. The MDS must ensure that any incidents or first aid given is recorded in the first aid book and a class communication note is completed for the teacher, so all parties are informed. In an emergency, an ambulance is called and members of SMT must be notified

SAFEGUARDING (Ref Safeguarding Policy, Health and Safety, Code of Conduct)

All Midday Supervisors should complete the Safeguarding Training on appointment at the school and at regular intervals after this. MDSs will complete Level One safeguarding training as soon as possible after their appointment All safeguarding referrals should be completed on the relevant form and passed to the designated officer straight away. In the absence of the designated officer, a member of SMT should be informed.

## *Resources*

- Boxes of indoor games.
- List of available therapies (passes needed) and lunchtime rota displayed on the staff notice board and hall door.
- Outdoor apparatus, games/bikes/football equipment kept in the outdoor sheds/rooms.

This policy should be read in conjunction with other School Policies and guidance documents, including job descriptions for those involved in lunchtime supervision and those relating to equal opportunities, health and safety, behaviour, safeguarding, First Aid and the School Staff Handbook.

Our intention is that during the designated lunch break children will have a safe, happy and worthwhile break from school teaching sessions in the middle of the day. The experience should be positive, and students will be supported by supervisory assistants, teaching support and teaching staff. Teaching staff, in line with union policy, oversee lunchtime on a voluntary basis and are given a free lunch on that day.

Appraisal and training The appraisal process is completed in line with the Appraisal Process for Support Staff. Targets are set and reviewed accordingly. Training will take place on a term basis and address the needs of the school as well as the individual. Communication for MDS can be found in the staffroom on the notice board and housekeeping meetings between the Senior MDS and SMT are held fortnightly.

Our school is a Rights Respecting school. This policy highlights these rights of the child:

Article 1 Every child under the age of 18 has all the rights in the Convention

Article 29 Education must develop every child's personality, talents and abilities to the full

Article 31 Every child has the right to relax, play and take part in a wide range of cultural and artistic activities

| Lunchtime Play Risk assessment | | |
|---|---|---|
| | Risk/Concern | Precautions |
| VENUE<br>Key Stage 2 yard:<br>Swing | Students falling off swing/students being hit by swing | Students to be supervised on swings. Adults to make swing go higher or lower by holding chains. Students to stand well away from swing area while waiting for turn |

| Open space | tripping over, grazing skin, injuries from playground equipment | Students to be supervised by an adult. Students to be encouraged to use equipment appropriately |
|---|---|---|
| KS2 2nd yard: Climbing frame | slipping/falling | Students to be supervised on climbing frame. Students encouraged to move steadily. Policy &RA. |
| PUPIL<br>J R | Mouthing sticks<br>Experiences a seizure | Adult to discourage<br>JW/CJ/CJ on care plan. Mid-day supervisors (MDS) to carry buzzer. Location of medication known by all staff 1:1 supervision to be maintained. |
| K P | Loses balance/trips/falls/bangs head/ walks into path of students or moving objects<br>Experiences a seizure | MDS to carry buzzer. Staff aware of possibility<br>Blankets to be used to keep in body heat Not to be exposed to extremely cold weather in winter months. |
| I R | Breathing becomes rattly/bubbly Positioning of wheelchair- set in the path of moving objects<br>Experiences a seizure | Manual handling plan to be adhered to. IR to have opportunity to enjoy playground Emergency action from care plan to be followed<br>(J Jones assigned as health worker). MDS to carry buzzer |

# RESOURCE: Sensory profile example

| Speech | Tactile | MobilityVestibular/Balance |
|---|---|---|
| I do not speak but communicate through...<br>• Eye contact & smiles<br>• PECS symbols - I can choose from 4 coloured symbols & am learning to *travel* with these.<br> • I am also learning to use a big mac switch to say "hello" | • I am sensitive to certain fabrics. Insists on wearing the same clothes<br>• I have difficulty standing close to other children | • I frequently twirl, spin myself throughout day<br>• I like to rock in chair/ on floor<br>**Proprioception/Body Awareness**<br>I chew on toys/clothes more than other children, I am clumsy, I bump into people and objects |
| **Auditory**<br>• I cannot concentrate, I am easily distracted by background noises<br>• I sometimes hold my hands over my ears to protect ears from sound | **Sensory Profile**<br>PHOTO OF ME | **Smell/Taste**<br>I can show distress at certain food smells<br>• I avoid trying new foods<br>• I have a restricted diet |
| **Things I like**<br>• Pairs of items, or things that go together<br>• Relaxing in the dark & soft play rooms | **Things I do not like...**<br>• To be rushed<br>• I often do not want to go outside to play, (this could be related to sun-shine affecting eyes)<br>• Transition times are diffi-cult for me. I need music cues | **Visual**<br>• I am easily distracted by nearby visual stimuli<br>• I cover my eyes if class-room lights on/affected by bright lights<br>• I prefer dimmed lighting |

# RESOURCE: Individual Education Plan (IEP)

| Name: | | Term: |
|---|---|---|
| | | |
| | | |
| Class: | | Teacher: |
| **English** | | |
| | | |
| **Maths** | | |
| | | |
| **PHSE** | | |
| | | |
| **Digital Competence** | | |
| | | |
| **Literacy and Numeracy Framework** | | |
| Literacy | | |
| Numeracy | | |
| | | |

| | |
|---|---|
| Student uses a TEACCH Station | Y |
| | |
| Student has an Individual Behaviour Plan | Y |

# RESOURCE: DIR floor time intervention report

D I R floor time has now been running for 4 weeks. Students who access DIR on a full-time basis are H R, J W and L S. Drop in sessions are offered to A M, R D, T M and L E.

## Staffing

There are three members of staff in the morning sessions and three in the afternoon sessions, M P, a HLTA, leads the sessions. Teacher's responsible for the students complete the IEP and set targets for the staff to follow.

The students who drop in have staff from their respective classes with them and have targets to work on set by their teachers.

## Individual student responses' to the DIR intervention

Students have responded extremely positively to this intervention and their emotional well-being has improved:

H R is now happier, much calmer, interacts well with the other pupils, has time to communicate his needs and as the room is less busy, he is able to cope better and manage his behaviour more positively. He prefers to learn via technology. He access's the white board activities independently, types in the title of his favourite songs on You Tube sits and listens to them. He now follows instructions from staff and interacts well with his peers.

Some slight behaviours still present themselves – mainly spitting – but staff have commented that they feel this is a form of communication. However, H may hit out when his needs/demands are not met straight away. Having spoken with parents, this seems to be learned behaviour. This is something that will be worked on at home and in school.

H is working towards turn taking and sharing.

J W is much happier and as a result much calmer. He is given his own space, and this has lowered his levels of anxiety. He interacts with pupils, listens and follows instructions. J is starting to become more verbal; asking his friends to play, asking for juice and biscuits. J is now more focussed on his play activities. He interacts and responds to adult interactions and that of his peers. As he is able to access the outdoor play area and garden, which is his preferred area for learning, he has now stopped trying to abscond.

Toileting was an issue for J Staff have worked hard at understanding his sensory profile and he now goes to the changing area with no issues.

J is working towards sharing, using PECs, or vocalising his needs instead of pushing. He is trying different foods and seeing continued success with his toileting needs.

L S is more relaxed and happier since joining DIR. L plays well with his peers, shares activities, asks for help and now offers help to others. His listening and concentration levels have improved; he also tolerates his peers and is more patient when he is engaged in play with them. L appreciates the quiet, calm environment of the class. He prefers to learn through a play-based approach at the moment, particularly construction. L still needs support to finish his tasks and to tidy them away.

L is working towards staying safe, using a quiet voice and a gentle approach.

All students attend their individual therapy sessions that support their individual sensory profiles.

## Staff comments

Staff are pleased that DIR time is a success for the students and their hard work is now paying dividends the results are positive with regards to the behaviours and students engagements with play.

Therapists have commented students are more engaged and calmer in their sessions and have seen huge improvements in their concentration.

Parents have all commented favourably on the difference DIR has made to the family.

## Drop-in sessions

Students who access the drop-in sessions have had various success rates. Staff have commented that a period of settling into the routine of attending the DIR floor time sessions has been an issue hopefully with time this will improve.

Staff supporting the drop-in sessions have been asked to provide picture cues for those students attending from their class. These have had a positive effect already as students are adjusting to the change.

Recommendations for Provision

- Staff training
- Class Teachers to provide Individual Support documents for DIR, i.e., IEP's
- DIR staff to have regular meetings with class teachers
- DIR staff to have regular meetings with parents
- Ongoing support from the behaviour coordinator and department heads
- Correct staff ratio maintained

B D
Behaviour Coordinator

# RESOURCE: DIR floortime™ policy

This policy explains the nature and use of DIR Floortime within a special school and its contribution to the education of students at that special school. This policy has been shared and approved by the teaching staff and school governors.

## Ethos

Our special school is committed to providing access to learning for all students with a diagnosis of Autism, ADHD, CLDD, PMLD, SLD and other special needs. All of our students have information processing difficulties. We provide high quality services and support to enable them to participate in a wide range of everyday learning and leisure activities. Our special school believes that all students and their families should have access to effective support from the school and staff should have the necessary knowledge and skills to work effectively with all students in our care. All students with learning differences are best viewed in terms of individual differences regardless of their diagnosis.

## Objectives

To value and respect the way our students learn best. Our special school's main objectives for preparing to use and using DIR Floortime are:

- To recognise and seek to maximise every student's potential who may need to use DIR Floortime
- Create individual profiles based on continuous assessment to determine a DIR intervention plan
- To raise awareness and develop confidence in the knowledge of students who need a different approach to learning.
- To ensure that DIR Floortime is supported by developing a shared knowledge, skills and understanding for staff of where each student is developmental.
- To develop appropriate strategies for interaction ad engagement.
- To acknowledge the need to work collaboratively with students and their families to deliver DIR Floortime.

## Rationale

Structure, visual support and individualised strategies appropriate for everyone are provided to aid all students access to the curriculum.

Most of our students have the following issues.

1. Social Interaction Impairment: Understand and use non-verbal and verbal communication (for example, not fully understanding the meaning of gestures, facial expressions or tone of voice).
2. Social Communication Impairment: Understand social behaviour that affects their ability to interact with children, young people and adults (for example have a literal understanding of language).
3. Social Imagination Impairment: (flexibility of thought and behaviour) (may be shown in restricted, obsessional or repetitive activities, a limited imagination and/or difficulty with change).

Many of our students have sensory processing problems and may have a different perception of sounds, sights, smell, touch and taste, which affects their response to these sensations. They may also have motor and planning difficulties and unusual sleep patterns, and all of these can affect their behaviour.

## What is DIR floortime ™?

It is a developmental, individual-differences and relationship-based systematic approach to helping students climb the developmental ladder.

DIR Floortime is most utilised for students with educational, social-emotional, mental health and/or developmental challenges at our school. More information can be found in the book by Greenspan and Weider (1998).

The objectives of the DIR Model are to adjust the environment to meet the student's needs rather than focusing on compliance and isolated behaviours. Creating an environment where the student can be successful. The focus is on personal self-determined learning driven by the students own interests.

The D (Developmental) part of the Model Understanding where the child is developmentally is critical to planning a programme. The six developmental levels describe the developmental milestones that every child must master for healthy emotional and intellectual growth. Through play we want our students to use their own ideas to communicate needs and think and play creatively. These developmental capacities are essential for spontaneous and empathic relationships as well as the mastery of academic skills.

The I (Individual differences) part of the Model describes the unique biologically based ways each child takes in, regulates, responds to and comprehends sensations such as sound, touch and the planning and sequencing of actions and ideas. Sensory profiling is essential.

The R (Relationship-based) part of the Model describes the learning relationships with teachers, teaching assistants and peers who tailor their interactions to the child's individual differences and developmental capacities to enable progress in mastering the essential foundations.

DIR Floortime emphasises the critical role of parents and other family members because of the importance of their emotional relationships with their child.

The DIR Model is a comprehensive framework that enables teachers to construct a plan tailored to the student's unique challenges and strengths.

At our school, in addition to Floortime, we include numerous therapeutic interventions alongside.

## The six developmental levels

The six developmental levels describe the developmental milestones that every child must master for healthy emotional and intellectual growth.

*Level 1: Self-regulation and interest in the world – goal: becoming calm, attentive and interested in the world.*

Staff have to understand each sensory profile to be able to meet those sensory needs. To help your student feel comfortable in the world you must first carefully observe which sensations help your student become calm and regulated, which ones overwhelm them, and put them in a state of flight, fright, freeze or appease.

*Level 2: Form warm engagements with others*

Through observing your student's interests and natural desires, you will understand what they find enjoyable, what motivates them. The only way you can engage your student at the beginning is by joining their interests, regardless of how unusual they are. Then gradually expand out from that base of security. Anytime your student becomes withdrawn or overexcited and irritable, you need to go back to the baseline and expand more slowly.

*Level 3: Two-way communication*

Your student's interest and purpose are the first step in meaningful communication and reciprocal actions. You want your student to OPEN the circle of communication and CLOSE the circle. Getting to a continuous back-and-forth communication is the goal of this stage.

*Level 4: Sustained interaction*

Challenge your student to persist in their interactions with you to solve problems - not only those that they want to figure out on their own, but also those that you present to them.

*Level 5: Symbolic creative thinking*

Join in with make-believe play.

*Level 6: Logical thinking*

Challenge your student to consider the opinion of others.

## Learning to think

Help your student learn to think by holding long conversations with them in which you seek their opinions. Remember to keep asking "Why?"

All people continue to develop throughout life. There are as many as ten more levels. For more support with these higher levels read Greenspan and Weider (1998).

# Entitlement

We endorse the aims of the National Curriculum to provide a broad and balanced curriculum and deliver the DIR Floortime to enable students to access the curriculum.

# Implementation

**Foundation Department –** *Two students in the department currently attend full-time in the DIR Floortime room. IEPs are set by the class teachers using an assessment tool. Students are then put into their Functional Emotional Development Levels based on these IEPs. A programme of activities is then put in place by the class teacher in line with the DIR Floortime approach. Teaching Assistants take observation notes and photos, which are available for the class teachers to assess their students' progress.*

 **Key Stage Two –** *Three students in the department currently attend full-time in the DIR Floortime Room. IEPs are set by the class teachers using an assessment tool. Students are then put into their Functional Emotional Development Levels based on these IEPs. A programme of activities is then put in place by the class teacher in line with the DIR Floortime approach.*

 *Other students may attend for some individual sessions during the morning if class teachers feel they would benefit from this approach. They are the responsibility of the class teachers, who follow the DIR Floortime guidance.*

 *DIR Floortime is also delivered to students as part of the playing and being with others curriculum throughout the school.*

# Planning

Class teachers write individual educational plans (IEPs) using the school assessment tool. Students are then put into their Functional Emotional Development Levels based on these IEPs. A programme of activities is then put in place by the class teacher in line with the DIR Floortime approach. The class teacher may also choose targets that support the well-being of the student. Class teachers set different targets to meet the specific needs of individual students.

# Resources

The DIR Floortime Room has a variety of areas with resources in that support the activities found in the six developmental levels. Class teachers also use their play skills areas for when they are delivering DIR Floortime in their classrooms.

 The HLTA leads the development of a central bank of resources needed for DIR Floortime strategies that class teachers may access via the schools website.

## *Training*

At our special school, there is a commitment to training all teaching staff and the HLTA responsible for the DIR classroom in DIR floortime™. To give awareness-raising training to all Teaching Assistants. Training is available to all staff members at our special school in the following way,

- Induction Basic Autism Awareness Training
- Two-day DIR Floortime™ training course
- DIR Floortime™ training as part of our CPD Rolling Programme

## *Equal opportunities*

DIR Floortime is delivered to students regardless of gender, culture or ability. Boys and girls have equal access to this approach.

## *Monitoring and evaluation of DIR floortime*

The Head Teacher carries out detailed monitoring and evaluation of the Nursey and Foundation Phase and the Key Stage Two departments, which includes the delivery of DIR Floortime within these departments. Monitoring and evaluation are carried out on a rolling programme every two years. As part of this process, the Head Teacher looks at all aspects of how DIR Floortime is delivered in school and its relationship to student progress. An action plan for further development is then drawn up.

## *Supervision*

The HLTA for DIR and all class teachers have overall responsibility for the supervision of all those receiving the DIR Floortime. The class teacher will evaluate student's suitability to access the delivery of the DIR Floortime room and may request the advice of SMT members for support.

## *Other guidance*

As a Rights Respecting School, we are committed to embedding the principles and values of the United Nations Convention for the Rights of the Child (UNCRC). This policy ensures that our students have access to and are supported in the following articles of the convention.

| Article 1 | Every child under the age of 18 has all the rights in the Convention |
| --- | --- |
| Article 29 | Education must develop every child's personality, talents, and abilities to the full |
| Article 31 | Every child has the right to relax, play and take part in a wide range of cultural and artistic activities |
| Article 42 | Every child has the right to know their rights |

# RESOURCE: Impact report on play therapy

| | The Impact of Therapeutic Play at our school. |
|---|---|

## Information about the sessions

Therapeutic Play at our school is run by a Play Therapist who is also a teacher on the school staff. She is on the Play Therapy UK standards register and runs the sessions according to their specific guidelines, including a code of confidentiality.

Therapeutic Play is psychotherapeutic in nature. It is non-judgmental and non-directed. The aim is to enable children to address their own issues and be able to express themselves in a safe environment with an adult they trust. Hence the child directs the play so they can process issues that may be impacting on their emotional understanding as well as their age-appropriate development.

## Agreed aims for therapeutic play

Parents and/or the teacher who referred the child are invited to give between one and four aims for the sessions. School-based aims tend to be taken from their Individual Education Plan (IEP), maybe their individual behaviour plan (IBP) and their Annual Targets. Although the therapist does not structure the sessions to meet these aims, she works on a one-to-one basis with the children and so is able to feed back any relevant observations to the class teachers. She selects targets related to social and communication skills from the child's assessment profile.

The aims set by all the parents to date have related to the child's well-being such as 'help to reduce his feelings of anxiety', 'improve her confidence', and 'for him to be happy in school'. While these can be difficult concepts to measure our findings at Pen Coch have been positive. By permitting the child to lead the session and only joining in when invited to do so the adult empowers the child.

## The children

Eight students have taken part in the sessions to date. Seven of them have a diagnosis of autism spectrum disorder, and one has a diagnosis of ADHD. As a trainee, the practitioner can only take children who have a moderate level of need as determined by PTUK. The Goodman 'Strengths and Difficulties Questionnaire' is used to decide this level. Parents and the class teacher are invited to complete the questionnaire before the sessions commence and after they have finished. This highlights any significant changes that may have occurred in the child's behaviour.

## School targets achieved to date

Targets are said to be achieved if they occurred naturally on a minimum of three occasions. The following table gives some indication of the impact of therapeutic play at our school.

- To date 76% of the targets set have been achieved. Four pupils* are still currently working on their targets.
- One student** missed a substantial amount of sessions due to illness but will be included in the next set of sessions.
- Children were not all set the same number of PSHE, Citizenship and Oracy targets.
- More Citizenship targets were achieved than in the other subjects.
- There were many positive changes in patterns of play, behaviour and social interaction that are not accounted for in this specific set of targets.
- SDQs completed by class teachers and parents at the end of the first set of four students all showed some progress, although it is not guaranteed that this is a direct result of therapeutic play.
- All children attending came willingly when offered a choice.
- When the first set of four children finished their sessions, they all expressed regret that the sessions were now ending.
- One of the initial four children has since reported that he refers to his personal therapeutic story when he is feeling stressed.
- One of the initial four children has since demonstrated how he used his 'calming breaths' in a stressful situation.
- Three students initially found it difficult to settle into a situation in which they were not being directed. However, within a short period of time, all showed signs of increased confidence and use of initiative.
- One student's play was initially focussed on themes of chaos and was aggressive, but gradually changed over the weeks. In the final sessions, his more violent characters had left their gang and were taking bubble baths and singing on 'YouTube'
- One child spoke constantly in an Americanised television voice in his first sessions. He then went through a short period in which he was extremely peaceful during his sessions. He rarely spoke but was engaged in very calm sensory activities of his own choosing. In his final sessions, he began to speak more naturally in his own voice.
- One child revealed his extreme anxiety about forthcoming hospital appointments. He responded well to a therapeutic story on this theme.
- All sessions were monitored by the PTUK supervisor who has consistently given positive feedback to the therapist.

| Targets by Individuals | | | | |
|---|---|---|---|---|
| Child | Total Number of Targets Set | Targets Achieved | Progress Made or Ongoing Targets | No Progress Made |
| BM** | 4 | 1 | 3 | |
| BE | 4 | 4 | | |
| FM | 4 | 4 | | |
| ME | 4 | 4 | | |
| MM* | 4 | 2 | 2 | |
| RH* | 4 | 2 | 2 | |
| MJ* | 5 | 4 | 1 | |
| GE* | 4 | 4 | | |
| TOTALS | 33 | 25 | 8 | |
| **Targets by Subject** | | | | |
| Oracy/Expressive Communication | P.S.H.E. | | Citizenship | |
| 9 | 6 | | 6 | |

## Conclusion

All the students involved (and the therapist) enjoyed the sessions. The biggest obstacle faced by the therapist is the interruptions to the sessions due to school holidays, ill health and timetable changes. Our school also provides DIR floortime and Venture into Play to ensure all students have an opportunity for therapeutic play.

# RESOURCE:  Soft play rules

The Soft Play Room remains locked unless a scheduled session with adequate and responsible staff is taking place

Have fun but remember

Shoes are not allowed. Socks only

No food, drink or glasses allowed

Students to visit the toilet before using the Soft Play room

Appropriate clothing must be worn

Staff should not use the Soft Play equipment. Supervise or assist only.

Students suffering an injury cannot use Soft Play

Remove loose or sharp objects before entering Soft Play

Sessions have time limits. Please abide by these.

Report accidents or incidents immediately and complete the necessary paperwork

Any damage to the room is to be reported to the caretaker and senior management and the room to be locked until suitable for use.

*Risk Assessments*

| Directorate | | | Activity (Brief Description) | | Soft Play | |
|---|---|---|---|---|---|---|
| **Service** | Education | | **People at Risk** | | Students and Staff | |
| **Location** | School | | **Date** | | **Review Date** | ongoing |
| **Assessor** | | | **Issue Number** | | 1 | |
| **Item No** | Hazard (Include Defects) | RISK RATING (Without controls) High/Medium/Low | Existing Control Measures | | | RISK RATING (With existing controls) High/Medium/Low |
| | **Injury through items** | Medium | All shoes, glasses, jewellery, badges, belts, keyrings, and any sharp objects must be removed before using the Soft Play- room. | | | Low |
| | Cleanliness and tidinessTripping | | Equipment list kept by caretaker and cleaning staff and regular maintenance checks undertaken. Balls in ball pool regularly part of the school cleaning process | | | |
| | **Lone working** Working in Soft Play room alone/in an isolated location | Medium | Only agreed tasks to be undertaken. Reduced time spent working alone so far is reasonably practicable. Consideration given to staff at increased risk and lone working activities avoided where practicable. If practicable insert CCTV. | | | Low |
| | | | No food, drinks, balloons, glitter or | | | Low |

134

(Continued)

| | | | |
|---|---|---|---|
| **Choking** | Medium | similar are permitted in the Soft play-room. Ensure students do not put balls from ball-pool into their mouths. This is for hygiene reasons as well as H&S. Ensure broken balls are removed immediately from room. | |
| **Behavioural Issues** | High | Pupil's individual behaviour plan (IBP) in individual folder and followed by staff. Staff aware of pupil's IBP. Staff trained in positive behaviour strategies and de-escalation techniques. Regular review of risk assessments of individual students before beginning Soft Play. | Low |
| **Medical Issues** | Medium | Students care plans in place and followed by staff. Staff aware of pupil's medical needs and rescue meds taken to Venturing into Play- room. Staff trained in medical needs determine whether student fit to attend that particular session of Soft Play. Adequate staffing required or Soft Play is cancelled | |
| **Danger of unnecessary injury** | High | Ensure students have plenty of room. Vigilant supervision to ensure behaviours under control. Supervisor of Soft Play ensures students are in similar size groupings. Supervisor of Soft Play is responsibly | Low |

(Continued)

| | | Risk |
|---|---|---|
| **Injury through lack of supervision** | ensuring that all students are behaving in an appropriate, safe, and controlled manner. Supervising adults must intervene to control a potentially dangerous situation for the safety and well-being of all involved. | Low |
| **Overcrowding** | | |
| **Large students colliding with smaller students** | Medium | |
| **Overenthusiastic students** | Medium | |
| | In the event that someone is seriously injured remove all other students in a calm, controlled manner. Do not move student. Phone 999 immediately and follow instructions. Inform parents. Complete accident form and medical records. | Low |
| **Emergency** | High | |

**FURTHER ACTION REQUIRED TO REDUCE RISKS TO ACCEPTABLE LEVEL**

| | | |
|---|---|---|
| Consideration given to staff at increased risk i.e., new, or expectant mothers, inexperienced staff etc. and lone working activities avoided where practicable. | | |
| Risk Assessments of individual students behavioural needs carried out beforehand. | | |
| Risk Assessments of individual students medical needs carried out beforehand | | |
| *Ultimate Risk* | *HIGH* | *Ultimate Existing Risk* | *LOW* |

| Item No | Further Action necessary to control risk | Action By | Date Completed | RESIDUAL RISK (With further controls) High/Medium/Low |
|---|---|---|---|---|
| Assessor(s) Signature(s) | Managers Name | | Manager Signature | |
| Other relevant RiskAssessments: | | | | |

| | | | |
|---|---|---|---|
| **Directorate** | Ms A Anderson | **Activity (Brief Description)** | LEGO Club therapy |
| **Service** | Education | **People at Risk** | Students and Staff |
| **Location** | | **Date** | **Review Date** | ongoing |
| **Assessor** | | **Issue Number** | 1 |

| Item No | Hazard (Include Defects) | RISK RATING (Without controls) High/Medium/Low | Existing Control Measures | RISK RATING (With existing controls) High/Medium/Low |
|---|---|---|---|---|
| | **General Storage**<br>Falling objects<br>Not secured, poorly installed.<br>Sited too high/overloaded | Medium | Storage unit properly installed and fixings in place.<br>Storage to be organised.<br>Restricted access to students.<br>Controlled limits of items stored. | Low |
| | Cleanliness and tidiness<br>Tripping<br>Struck by falling object | Medium | Rubbish is regularly removed.<br>Equipment tided away after activity has finished.<br>General tidy of room at the end of the day. | Low |
| | **Lone working**<br>Working in LEGO® Club room alone/in an isolated location<br>Accident, injury, delayed assistance in emergency | Medium | Only agreed tasks to be undertaken.<br>Reduced time spent working alone so far is reasonably practicable.<br>Consideration given to staff at increased risk and lone working activities avoided where practicable. | Low |

| | | | |
|---|---|---|---|
| Choking on LEGO pieces | High | Room is nearby to other classrooms in the event of summoning assistance. This room also has inbuilt CCTV. Staff support throughout therapy activities. Students reminded of therapy rules. Staff trained in basic first aid. Adequate staff required if necessary Medical risk assessments of individual students carried out before beginning the therapy if this is a known behaviour by student. | Low |
| Behavioural Issues | Medium | Students IBP in individual folder and followed by staff. Staff aware of student's IBP. Staff trained in positive behaviour strategies and de-escalation techniques. Adequate staffing required if necessary Risk Assessments of individual students carried out before beginning therapy. Students care plans in place and followed by staff. Staff aware of pupil's medical needs and rescue meds taken to therapy room. | Low |

(Continued)

*(Continued)*

| | | |
|---|---|---|
| **Medical Issues** | High | Staff trained in medical needs.<br>Adequate staffing required if necessary<br>Risk Assessments of individual<br>students carried out before beginning<br>therapy. |
| | | Low |

## FURTHER ACTION REQUIRED TO REDUCE RISKS TO ACCEPTABLE LEVEL

Consideration given to staff at increased risk i.e., new, or expectant mothers, inexperienced staff etc. and lone working activities avoided where practicable.

| | HIGH | Ultimate Existing Risk | LOW |
|---|---|---|---|
| Ultimate Risk | | | |

| Item No | Further Action necessary to control risk | Action By | Date Completed | RESIDUAL RISK (With further controls) High/ Medium/Low |
|---|---|---|---|---|
| Assessor(s) Signature(s) | Managers Name | | Manager Signature | |
| Other relevant Risk Assessments: | | | | |

| Directorate | | | Activity (Brief Description) | | Venturing into Play | |
|---|---|---|---|---|---|---|
| Service | Education | | People at Risk | | Students and Staff | |
| Location | School | | Date | Nov15 | Review Date | ongoing |
| Assessor | | | Issue Number | 1 | | |
| Item No | Hazard (Include Defects) | RISK RATING (Without controls) High/Medium/Low | Existing Control Measures | | | RISK RATING (With existing controls) High/Medium/Low |
| | **General Storage** Falling objects Not secured, poorly installed. Sited too high/overloaded | Medium | Storage unit properly installed and fixings in place. Storage to be organised. Restricted access to pupils. Controlled limits of items stored. | | | Low |
| | Cleanliness and tidiness Tripping Struck by falling object | Medium | Rubbish is regularly removed. Equipment tidied away after activity has finished General tidy of Venturing into Play room at the end of the day. | | | Low |
| | **Lone working** Working in VIP room alone/ in an isolated location Accident, injury, delayed assistance in emergency | Medium | Only agreed tasks to be undertaken. Consideration given to staff at increased risk and lone working activities avoided where practicable. | | | Low |

| Hazard | Risk | Control Measures | Residual Risk |
|---|---|---|---|
| | | Venturing into Play room has indoor CCTV. | Low |
| **Choking on Venturing into Play pieces** | High | Staff support throughout Venturing into Play activities. | Low |
| | | Staff trained in basic first aid. Adequate staff given if necessary Venturing into Play room is near other classroom where staff are onsite in the event of summoning assistance. | Low |
| | | Risk Assessments of individual students carried out before beginning Venturing into Play Therapy by class teacher if this is a known behaviour by pupil. | Low |
| **Behavioural Issues** | Medium | Students IBP in individual folder and followed by staff. Staff aware of pupil's IBP. Staff trained in positive behaviour strategies and de-escalation techniques. Adequate staffing Risk Assessments of individual students carried out before beginning Venturing into Play. | Medium |

(Continued)

*(Continued)*

| Medical Issues | | |
|---|---|---|
| | High | Students care plans in place and followed by staff. Staff aware of pupil's medical needs and rescue meds accompany Staff trained in medical needs. Adequate staffing provided Risk Assessments of individual students carried out beforehand Venturing into Play room is near other classrooms where staff are onsite in the event of summoning assistance |
| | | |

144

## FURTHER ACTION REQUIRED TO REDUCE RISKS TO ACCEPTABLE LEVEL

| | | HIGH | Ultimate Existing Risk | LOW |
|---|---|---|---|---|
| Consideration given to staff at increased risk i.e., new, or expectant mothers, inexperienced staff etc. and lone working activities avoided where practicable. | | | | |
| Ultimate Risk | | | | |

| Item No | Further Action necessary to control risk | Action By | Date Completed | RESIDUAL RISK (With further controls) High/Medium/Low |
|---|---|---|---|---|
| Assessor(s) Signature(s) | Managers Name | | Manager Signature | |
| Other relevant Risk Assessments: | | | | |

# RESOURCE: Venture into Play policy

Reviewed date: ...................

This policy explains the nature of Venturing into Play within the school and its contribution to the education of students at our school.

This policy has been shared and approved by the teaching staff and school governors.

## *Aims*

Venturing into Play offers students the opportunity to:

- To explore and practice play and social skills
- To help them to make friends and learn about their ever-expanding world
- To encourage confidence and concentration
- To foster their imagination and creativity
- To support emotional healing and growth

Venturing into Play should be a personal and pleasurable experience, which enriches the lives of the students and those around them.

## *What is Venturing into Play?*

Venturing into Play (VIP) is a play skills profile for children with learning differences. It was developed by Dr Caroline Smith.

The VIP Play Skills Profile (VIP) provides a practical tool for those working with children with learning differences. Originally based on the detailed observations of the play of children diagnosed with autism and a clear understanding of the play of typically developing children. The VIP Play skills profile considers both the social and cognitive developmental dimensions of play. It provides a tool for developing important baseline statements about both the social interactions and the developmental levels of children with learning differences. On the social dimensions, it offers 34 statements about how the child joins with others to play, ranging from isolated play to initiating the play with groups of children. On the developmental dimensions, it offers 26 statements ranging from sensory-motor play to the early stages of sociodramatic play. We have successfully used VIP with students with learning differences.

Subject to extensive use and revision by experienced staff working in mainstream and special schools the VIP provides an accessible tool for accurately describing the play, setting targets and identifying the student's rate of progress.

Each VIP offers a usable resource to complete for a named child. It has proved helpful in recording the progress of children with severe learning difficulties and autism

The VIP Play Skills Profile is a useful resource for, parents, carers, speech and language therapists, health visitors, clinical and educational psychologists, teachers, SENCOs, teaching assistants and those working in pre-school settings and those working with the developmental young in special schools.

The combination of practice based on sound theoretical knowledge, matched with a clear communication style, makes the VIP a practical and useful resource for a wide range of professionals.

## Suggestions for use

The VIP Play Skills Profile enables those working with a child with a learning difficulty to take a baseline; monitor and celebrate progress and to set long-term goals and shorter term targets.

The VIP Play Skills Profile does not aim to describe every step in the development of play for individual children, instead, it provides useful markers and signposts.

## Entitlement

We endorse the aims of the National Curriculum to provide a broad and balanced curriculum and deliver reflexology to enable students to access the curriculum.

## Planning

Teachers match educational targets, where possible from the school assessment profile. They share and discuss those targets with the Venturing into Play therapist/teaching assistant (TA). The Venturing into Play therapist and the teacher may also choose targets that support the well-being of the pupil. Teachers set different targets to meet the specific needs of individual students.

## Equal opportunities

Venturing into Play is delivered to students regardless of gender, culture or ability. Boys and girls have equal access to this therapy.

## Resources

Venturing into Play is delivered in a therapy room at the school by a Venturing into Play therapist/TA. The therapy room has a play skills area, which is resourced with a sand tray and miniatures, small world toys, aggressive and power toys, art toys, building and mastery toys, dolls and doll houses, books, games, musical instruments and role-play equipment.

Students have an initial first observational session where they can explore the room and the Venturing into Play skills therapist/TA makes observations of the child's play. A VIP Play Skills Profile is created based on these observations and the Venturing into Play therapist works through the markers/signposts as set in the VIP Play Skills Profile. The VIP Play Skills Profile includes Theme 1: The Social Dimension (Solitary Play, Adult Coming Alongside, Adult Getting in on play, getting others into the play, Getting Child–Child interaction) Theme 2: The Developmental Dimension (Sensory – motor play, Relational Play, Constructional Play, Cause and Effect Play, Functional/Representative Play, Symbolic Play, Sociodramtic Play).

During the beginning of each session students go through the Venturing into Play rules and format for the session. An object of reference/signifier is also used to aid the understanding of students. Students are prepared for Venturing into Play by a social story. During the end of each session students are prepared to leave the Venturing into Play room by a visual steps format and sand timer.

## Assessment, recording and reporting of student progress

Evaluation of learning outcomes comes from individual assessment planning and this evaluation is used to inform future planning. The Venturing into Play leader records the progress made by students towards their targets after each session and also records any evidence that the therapy has supported the well-being of the pupil. This recording sheet is copied and placed in an individual Venturing into Play class file. The class teacher uses this evidence to write end of session reports home to inform parents of the progress made by their child and also writes reports for each pupil's annual review.

An evaluation sheet is completed by the class teacher to show the impact of the therapy on the students learning and/or health.

## Monitoring and evaluation of venturing into play

The Therapies Consultant carries out detailed monitoring and evaluation of Venturing into Play. As part of the process, the consultant looks at all aspects of how Venturing into Play is delivered in school and its relationship to student progress. An action plan for further development is then drawn up. Monitoring and evaluation are carried out on a rolling programme every two years.

## Supervision

The Venturing into Play therapist and the school therapies consultant have overall responsibility for the supervision and general safety of all those receiving a therapeutic session of Venturing into Play.

The therapies consultant and VIP therapist will evaluate every application to assess the pupil's suitability to receive Venturing into Play.

## Data handling

It is essential that the VIP therapist maintains appropriate and detailed records. They must ensure they are kept confidentially and adhere to data protection legislation ensuring all records held are appropriate and stored securely.

## Health and hygiene

The VIP therapist must ensure they maintain a safe environment for their clients. The Venturing into Play room should be warm, clean, and comfortable and be free from all potential hazards.

## Risk assessments

A risk assessment should be carried out in respect of each student referred for Venturing into Play. This will include any mobility issues that may require the use of the hoist and an individual manual handling plan will be put in place if necessary. The screening forms will provide information relating to any behaviour and/or medical conditions the student may have to ensure these are taken into consideration. As the VIP therapist works alone with students, a phone is installed in the room to safeguard both the student and therapist. If a student has a medical condition that requires constant monitoring it may be deemed necessary for an additional member of staff to accompany the student to ensure their individual health needs are being met.

## Accident procedures

All accidents or incidents that occur whilst in the Venturing into Play room or on the way to or from the Venturing into Play room must be immediately reported to the Head Teacher and guidance sought from a qualified first aider if appropriate. An accident form should be obtained from the school office and completed timeously (within 24 hours of the incident/accident).

## Other guidance

It is appreciated that whilst every care may be taken to promote safety, they may be occasions and situations that occur despite safety precautions being in place. In such an eventuality further clarification and advice will be sought from the Head Teacher who may seek further guidance from the local authority.

As a Rights Respecting School we are committed to embedding the principles and values of the United Nations Convention for the Rights of the Child (UNCRC). This reflexology policy ensures that our students have access to and are supported in the following articles of the convention.

| Article 1 | Every child under the age of 18 has all the rights in the Convention |
|---|---|
| Article 29 | Education must develop every child's personality, talents, and abilities to the full |
| Article 31 | Every child has the right to relax, play and take part in a wide range of cultural and artistic activities |
| Article 42 | Every child has the right to know their rights |

# RESOURCE: Breakfast club assistant

Level 2: - To work under the direct instruction of senior staff assisting in the day-to-day organisation of the Breakfast Club, supervising and taking care of the children.

Support for the Pupils

- Provide a safe and secure atmosphere and relaxing environment for young children, and supervising children during the breakfast time period
- Setting up playrooms and tidying away at the end of sessions
- Encouraging full involvement and participation of young children
- Providing general supervision and scaffolding play
- Providing a range of food choices according to sensory dictates
- Adapting menus to suit children's needs/feed children if necessary
- Safely receive children from parents/carers and ensuring safe delivery of children to relevant classes
- Encouraging children to partake in eating their breakfast and the development of mealtime skills
- Encouraging children to participate in activities and appropriate behaviour with others
- Ensuring that the children clearly understand instructions fully
- Resolution of any issues/problems that may arise

Support for the Teacher

- Support Breakfast Supervisor in supervising play activities relevant to the children's care, physical, social and emotional development
- Inform teachers of any relevant information in relation to the welfare of the children

Support for the Curriculum

- Supervise guided play activities relevant to physical social and emotional development

Support for the School

- Responsible for the preparation of healthy breakfasts each day
- Maintaining an agreed standard of cleanliness and hygiene to ensure the well-being of the children and staff
- Responsible for washing crockery, setup and store away of tables and chairs daily
- Responsible for feeding those children that require feeding support
- Be aware of and comply with policies and procedures relating to child protection, health and safety, security and confidentiality and data protection, reporting all concerns to an appropriate person
- Contribute to the overall ethos/work/aims of the school
- Appreciate and support the role of other professionals

- Attend relevant meetings as required
- Participate in training and other learning activities and performance development as required
- Administering, monitoring and evaluating stock records

| Experience | Previous experience of working with children |
| --- | --- |
| Qualifications/ Training | Food Hygiene Certificate where required |
| Knowledge/Skills | Possess a level of numeracy and literacy sufficient to carry out the duties of the post |

Good level of interpersonal and communication skills at all levels
Understanding of relevant policies/codes of practice and awareness of relevant legislation
Knowledge of Health and Safety (Risk Assessments)
Good awareness and ability to exercise confidentiality where necessary

## *Breakfast supervisor*

Level 3: - To comply with all levels 2 requirements and in addition

- to be responsible for the development and daily management of the Breakfast Club, providing a safe, caring and stimulating environment for children.
- Supervising Breakfast Assistants, developing and maintaining high standards throughout to ensure the welfare of the children.
- Resolution of any problems or issues that may arise.
- Report any issues/serious problems regarding a child's behaviour to the Head Teacher
- Build links and work in partnership with parents, carers and professionals to promote the well-being of children
- Maintain the Breakfast Club to an agreed standard of cleanliness and hygiene, before, during and at the end of each session, to ensure the well-being of the children and staff
- Take a key role in suitably equipping the Breakfast Club in order to provide a stimulating environment for the children
- Ensure that high standards are maintained with regards to how the club runs, and participate in the recruitment and selection of Breakfast Club staff
- Administer, monitor and evaluate the number of places being used in order to maintain sustainability
- Maintain up to date records of incidents, attendance, resources and accurate financial records to ensure that financial procedures are adhered to
- Providing basic advice to parents/carers or clients of the Breakfast Club on the club's provisions, and signposting any enquiries not relating to the day to day operation of the club to the teacher, secretary or Head Teacher

- Responsible for the safekeeping of games/toys and all art/craft materials which are used in the club each day
- Be aware of and comply with policies and procedures relating to child protection, health and safety, security and confidentiality and data protection, reporting all concerns to an appropriate person
- Contribute to the overall ethos/work/aims of the school
- Appreciate and support the role of other professionals
- Attend relevant meetings as required
- Participate in training and other learning activities and performance development as required

| Experience | Previous experience of working with children |
|---|---|
| Qualifications / Training | Food Hygiene Certificate where required |
| Knowledge / Skills | Ability to organise, lead and motivate a team |

Good level of literacy and innumeracy sufficient to carry out the job tasks

Good level of interpersonal and communication skills at all levels

Knowledge of Health & Safety (Risk Assessments)

Full working knowledge of relevant policies/codes of practice/legislation

Good awareness and ability to exercise confidentiality where necessary

This job description should be read in conjunction with other School Policies and guidance documents, including job descriptions for those involved in lunchtime supervision and those relating to equal opportunities, health and safety, behaviour, safeguarding, First Aid and the School Staff Handbook.

All support staff are part of a whole school team. They are required to support the values and ethos of the school and school priorities as defined in the School Improvement Plan. This will mean focussing on the needs of colleagues, parents and students and being flexible in a busy pressurised environment.

This job profile sets out the duties of the post at the time it was drawn up. The post holder may be required from time to time to undertake other duties within the school as may be reasonably expected, without changing the general character of the duties or level of responsibility entailed. This is a common occurrence and would not justify a reconsideration of the grading of the post. It will be reviewed regularly and may be subject to modification or amendment after consultation with the post holder

# RESOURCE: Holiday play scheme resources

Policy for arrival and departure of children

## *Arrival*

1. Parents must notify the Club in good time re: attendance/non-attendance of their child. Unless exceptional circumstances apply, failure to give 24 hours' notice of cancellation/ non-attendance will incur the full cost of the session.
2. The parents and children will know the Club workers or individuals acting as support. All escorts will wear/carry identification and will have read and signed the Club's 'escort agreement'. In all circumstances, the support staff will have relevant police checks carried out.
3. The booking and payment of transport if via taxi will be the responsibility of the individual parents concerned and will be a private arrangement between the parents and the transport provider. However, the Club management recommends that the school, and children, will know the drivers of taxis and that proof of identity should be carried and produced if necessary. It is also highly recommended that parents insist on Criminal Records Checks be made on the taxi drivers involved.
4. Parents/carers will drop their children off at the Club's premises prompt to the time for which they have been booked in.

## *Departure*

1. Parents must collect their children by …. at the latest.
   Parents must give the names of all persons authorised to collect their child on the registration form. Only persons named on this form will be able to take the child from the Club unless prior arrangements in exceptional circumstances have been made known to the senior play worker/manager. A photo of this person should accompany the initial application or be sent by mobile in advance.
2. It is the responsibility of the parent/guardian to ensure that any changes to the named individuals who can collect their child are communicated to the play leader/manager both in writing, verbally and a photo sent by mobile.
3. The person collecting a child must approach a club worker so that club workers know who is being collected, and by whom, and can sign the children out.
4. If a parent is unreasonably late in collecting their child without contacting the Club to inform us of any unexpected delays – or is persistently late, a charge will be made at a rate of £5.00 for every half hour.
5. In the case of a parent/carer failing to collect the child, the Club co-ordinator will call the partner or emergency contact to come to the Club to take the child home. In the event of that person being unavailable, the child will be taken by play workers to the nearest police station.
6. No child will ever be left unsupervised because a parent/carer has failed to collect them.

## N.B.

Under the Children Act 1989, parents do not lose parental responsibility except through an adoption order. This means that divorced parents retain rights of contact with their children unless the courts have made an order that they should not do so. Play workers, therefore, do not have the right to stop divorced parents from collecting their children unless they are aware of a court order preventing contact between the parent and the children.

This situation would apply in the same way if the parents were in the process of separating. A mother's request that the children do not go home with their father cannot be guaranteed unless there is a court order preventing him from having contact with them.

Parental responsibility is given to both parents if they are married when the child is born or subsequently. Otherwise only the mother has parental responsibility. An unmarried father can acquire parental responsibility through a court application, as can a guardian, grandparents, etc.

Parent/carers should be in a FIT state to collect their children. If a parent/carer arrives in an "unfit" state, through, for example, alcohol or drug abuse, the senior play worker/manager cannot refuse to hand over the children but should tell the parent/carer that the police and/or Social Services Duty Officer will be informed immediately. The safety of the child is paramount.

## Children's participation policy

Children who can form their own views have the right to express those views and have them considered
**(Article 12, UN Convention on the Rights of the Child)**

## At our club

- All children in the Club will be treated with respect
- The children will be consulted on how the Club is set up and run
- Children will help devise and regularly review the ground rules of the Club
- A children's committee will be established to feedback ideas and comments to the play workers and adult committee members
- A suggestion box for the children will be prominently displayed for them to use
- Regular questionnaires will be given to the children and the results analysed and acted upon quickly
- Regular, informal children's meetings will be held to discuss issues on how the Club is run and activities that take place

A child who participates in decisions about our Club is likely to be happy and enthusiastic about being here – giving the working parent and carer peace of mind.

'A child who feels respected and valued by adults is likely to reciprocate that respect'.
*(Children's Participation Pack, Save the Children 1996)*

## Policy on missing children

There are a limited number of situations where a child could be missing, and these are:

1.  Where a child wanders off on an outing
2.  Where a child is missing from the agreed collection point on an outing

    A child is not able to escape from the premises. The premises are secure. The only time this could happen is during handover and it is the parents responsibility at handover.

Should a child become lost in circumstances as listed in points 1–2, the following action should be taken:

-   Make enquiries with relevant members of staff as to when the child was last seen and where.
-   Remember the safety of other children, with regard to supervision and security.
-   Ensuring that the remaining children are sufficiently supervised and secure, one or preferably two members of staff should search the building, outdoor premises and immediate vicinity.
-   If the child cannot be found within 15 minutes, then the Police and parents must be informed.
-   Continue to search, opening up the area, and keeping in touch with a mobile phone if available.
-   An incident form will be completed explaining exactly what happened. All the staff present, the child's parent/carer and the police should read and sign it.
-   When the situation has been resolved, members of staff should review the reasons for it happening and ensure measures are taken to make sure that it does not happen again.
-   The insurance company is notified.
-   The Care Standards Inspectorate for Wales is notified.

## Child missing from club collection point

-   If a child has been booked into the club, but is missing from the agreed collection point, the manager will be informed immediately
-   Any other children that have been collected should be kept calm and in one place while the search is carried out.
-   If the child is not found in the immediate school grounds, the following people will be contacted:

    a.  The parent/carer
    b.  The Police

-   An Incident Form will be completed explaining exactly what happened. All the staff present, the child's parent/carer and the police should read and sign it.
-   When the situation has been resolved, members of staff should review the reasons for it happening and ensure measures are taken to make sure that it does not happen again.

> The Insurance company is notified
>
> The Care Standards Inspectorate for Wales is notified.

## Statement of purpose

The Club is managed by a Voluntary Management Group which includes ....... An annual general meeting is held here.

### The aim

The aim of the Holiday Club is to provide quality accessible out of school childcare offering a range of play activities in a welcoming atmosphere.

### Numbers of children catered for

The scheme will operate for boys and girls aged 3–11 years. It is intended that the Club will cater for 30 children. The Club intends to offer a child-centred environment meeting the social physical, intellectual, creative and emotional needs of each individual child.

### Languages used

The main language of the Club will be English/Welsh/any other language. Bilingual signs will be used where appropriate.

### Opening hours

The Club will be open between 10am and 3.00 pm, Monday to Thursday, 1st Week of Easter Holidays and all 6 weeks of Summer Holidays.

### Contact information

Our contact address is School address

Tel: school telephone no.

We need to be aware of your contact details and have information regarding your children. Please complete the registration form and keep us informed of any change of details.

### Staff

There will be 11 qualified members of staff giving a ratio of 1 qualified staff to 2 children:

1. Senior manager: 2 Deputy Managers 18 Play workers. These may work part-time or job share during the time period specified.

Volunteers will assist at various times. All staff and volunteers will be DBS checked.

## Food

Snacks and drinks will be available during the sessions; this will be in line with our healthy eating policy, and to suit your child's dietary needs and preferences.

## Facilities

The facility will provide appropriate areas for a range of needs including a food preparation/ dining area, a quiet area, a large play area and outdoor play space. Toilet and first aid facilities will be available as well as personal storage and administrative space.

Activities will be planned weekly offering opportunities for free play. Children will be encouraged to participate in the planning of activities and ideas for equipment.

## Arrangements for complaints

The welfare of the boys and girls will be paramount, and we aim to meet the needs of both children and parent/carers. However, if there is cause for complaint at any time, please let the senior play worker know. We have a complaints procedure that is explained in the parent/carers handbook. If your complaint cannot be resolved, you are entitled to contact your local Care Standards Inspectorate for Wales office

Our parent/carers handbook sets out the Club's policies and we recommend that all users read this. Policies and procedures for the club are also available in the Club.

## Admissions policy

1. The summer Club is open to any child aged 3–11 years.
2. No child shall receive less favourable treatment on the grounds of race, colour, ethnic or national origin, religious beliefs and disability or in any other matter to do with the club.
3. In order to ensure fairness in the allocation of places, the following criteria will be taken into consideration:

- While available places exist, these will be allocated on a first come – first offer basis
- Then places will be given to children who are booking for every day of the week
- Then, first priority will be given to children of working parents/single working parents, parents who are studying, or training to re-enter the workforce
- Then siblings of children already at the Club will have priority over others
- Provision will be made for social services, employer or other sponsored places

4. Places can be reserved in advance in order to secure placements although payment is required on booking. Children cannot be admitted to the Club until the parent/carer formally registers them. Parents/carers are to provide all relevant contact details and information regarding any special requirements or needs of a child.

5. Parents/carers must notify play workers at the earliest opportunity if there are any changes to the children's registration details so that forms can be updated regularly.

6. Fees must be paid in advance when booking your child's place. This is not refundable. In exceptional circumstances, which will be determined by the management committee, credits may be offered.

7. If the Club is oversubscribed a waiting list will be kept and administered by the senior play worker/manager.

8. The management committee reserves the right to refuse admission to any child whose behaviour is, in our opinion, not in the best interest of the other children's health and safety. (This course of action would only be implemented once our agreed procedures for tackling behaviour problems have been exhausted).

9. Parents are required to sign a contract confirming that they have read and understood the policies and procedures outlined in the Parent's/Carer's Handbook and agree to abide by the terms and conditions of the Club.

10. Parent/carers must give one month's notice in writing to the management committee when they wish to terminate their contract with the Club.

## Child induction plan

1. On making an initial enquiry about using the setting the family will be provided with a 'statement of purpose'/information leaflet to give them key information about the Club's operation.

2. Should the family wish to proceed and make a booking then a full 'Club Handbook' will be provided to allow families to familiarise themselves with the Club's policies and procedures.

3. During this initial visit parents/carers can ask the manager about any queries they may have regarding the policies outlined in the handbook.

4. Parents/carers and children are welcome to look at the Clubs past projects/Scrapbook.

5. Children will be given a basic induction, which will include outlining the Club's ground rules and showing children around the premises (toilets, toy cupboard, out of bounds, areas etc.)

6. The manager will welcome all new children and introduce them to the Staff and other children at the Club.

7. Children are encouraged to make new friends and join in activities. However, the needs of the individual child will be respected, and no child forced to take part in any activity.

8. Parents will be informed of their child/children's progress and staff welcome questions from parents about their child.

## Play policy

This Club recognises that play is a vital component of a child's life. We will ensure that children have access to freely chosen, varied, child-centred play opportunities.

Within the framework of current legislation, we will aim to ensure that:

- The child will be the centre of the play process
- Children will be consulted and listened to, and their views acted upon where possible
- Play staff are responsive and help to enrich the children's play opportunities
- Play staff facilitate appropriate risk and increase children's awareness of their physical capabilities and limitations
- Play opportunities promote equality of opportunities and challenge discrimination
- Play opportunities will motivate children, increase self-esteem and foster positive attitudes
- Guided play will be offered at all times to support play development
- Quiet areas will be provided to allow for sensory overload
- "Parties recognise the rights of the child to rest and to leisure, to engage in play and recreational activities appropriate to the age of the child"

*The United Nations Convention on the Rights of the Child, Article 31*

"Play is nature's training for life"

*Lloyd George*

## Medication policy

If medication is to be given, the following practices will be followed:

- Medicines will not usually be administered unless they have been prescribed for that child by a doctor
- Medicines will be stored in their original containers, clearly labelled with the child's name and inaccessible to children
- Checks will be made to ensure that any medication received into the Club is not out of date
- The parent/carer will give prior written permission to administer any medication
- Written records will be kept of all medicines administered to children and parents/carers must sign the record book to acknowledge the entry
- If appropriate, details of the exact time any current medication was last administered to the child will be obtained

If the administration of prescription medicines requires technical/medical knowledge, then individual training will need to be provided for staff from a qualified health professional. Training will be specific to the individual child concerned.

The registered person will confirm that the administration of medication conforms to their insurance cover.

We recommend that hats and sunscreen are used when the children are playing outside in sunny weather. However, they will have to supply their own and apply their own sunscreen themselves.

## Special needs policy

### What are special needs?

There are many definitions of special needs that are appropriate for different purposes. Many children may be assessed as having a special need at some time in their school life. Children who need extra support in the classroom may have no special need within a play setting. Some children however may require specialist treatment, facilities or care while in the Club that is above and beyond the usual provision for most children.

### Special needs statement of intent

The Club aims to provide a welcoming and supportive environment for all children, staff and parents. They will all be treated with dignity and respect. Our school supports integration and the treatment of all children and adults as individuals, wherever this is possible.

- Where possible the Club will aim to provide adaptations to the facilities and environment in order to cater for individual special needs
- The individual needs of children will be considered when programme planning and buying toys and other equipment
- Where appropriate, children's progress will be monitored and recorded in consultation with parents and carers
- Staff will receive appropriate special needs training as required
- Full cooperation will be given to outside agencies in order to meet the specific needs of the child
- The Club will consult with children and parents as appropriate with regard to individual special needs
- Strategies such as positive behaviour management will be implemented
- The Club will promote anti-discriminatory practices and encourage a positive atmosphere for all
- If a child requires one to one support at the club, we will make every effort to work with the parents/carers and relevant organisations to access additional funding and extra staff members to provide one to one support

## Anti-bullying policy

While petty 'tale telling' is not desirable, genuine 'whistle-blowing' on bullying and other un-acceptable behaviour is actively encouraged from children, staff and parents.

The Holiday Play Club defines bullying as:

*'Verbal and/or physical intimidation, both direct & indirect, that makes an individual feel threatened or uncomfortable'.*

This policy relates to all staff, children and parents/carers linked to the Club.

Changes in behaviour that suggest a child is being bullied will be dealt with in the following way:

- The child will be comforted and encouraged to explain what has happened
- The play leader/manager will investigate the matter in a sensitive manner (see confidentiality policy)
- Where the bullying has been perpetrated by another child the play leader/manager will work in partnership with the child and their parents (where appropriate) to find a positive way forward
- Following the investigation, the Club's child protection policy and/or behaviour management policy may be implemented depending upon the source of bullying

Opportunities for discussion, information and resources on the subject of bullying will be used as an integral part of the Club's programme. Specific instances may also trigger discrete activities on the subject in order to raise children's awareness.

## Child protection policy

The Safeguarding Officer for club is .............

It is the responsibility of all adults who care for children to protect them from harm. In accordance with the All Wales Child Protection Procedures Our Club operates a child protection policy.

If any person has knowledge, concerns or suspicions that a child is suffering, has suffered or is likely to be at risk of harm from others, it is their responsibility to ensure that the concerns are referred to Social Services or the police, who have statutory duties and powers to investigate and intervene when necessary.

At least one member of our staff has received child protection training and training will be cascaded to all members of staff. All members of staff have been made aware of possible symptoms of children at risk and are aware of their responsibility to report concerns according to the All Wales Child Protection Procedures, a copy of which is kept on the premises. Concerns must be kept confidential to as few people who need to know.

If a parent or carer has concerns about a child, they should be advised to contact the local Social Services department directly.

This applies to the following circumstances:

- If a child or young person displays recognised signs of abuse
- If someone tells a member of staff that they or another child or young person is being abused
- If the behaviour of any adult (including colleagues and members of the public) towards children or young people causes concern

The procedures set out in the All Wales Child Protection Procedures will be followed in the event of suspected child abuse.

**Useful contact numbers**

| Social Services Departments | Child and Family Services: |
| | Emergency Duty Team |
| NSPCC | Child Protection Line |
| Childline | |

# Confidentiality policy

The group's work with children and families will sometimes bring them into contact with confidential information.

To ensure that all who use and work in the group can do so with confidence, confidentiality will be respected in the following ways:

- Parents/carers will have ready access to any files and records of their own children but will not have access to information about any other children
- Staff should not discuss individual children, other than for purposes of activity planning/ group management with anyone other than the parents/carers of that child
- Information given by parents/carers to the play leader/member of staff should not be passed to other adults without permission
- Any anxieties/evidence relating to a child's personal safety should be kept in a confidential file and should not be shared within the group (except with the staff and the committee Chair). The Area Child Protection Guidelines will be followed in such cases
- Issues to do with the employment of staff, whether paid or unpaid, should remain confidential to the people directly involved with making personnel decisions
- The safety and well-being of the child will be of paramount importance
- Volunteers/students are advised of our confidentiality policy and will be required to follow it at all times

# Equal opportunities policy

We recognise that certain groups and individuals in our society are discriminated against because of their race, colour, ethnic or national origin, gender, physical, sensory or mental disability, marital status, age, social class, religious belief, sexual orientation, employment status and if they are HIV positive.

Accordingly, we are strongly committed to positive action to remove/counter discrimination in all aspects of our work - in our practice as employers, in the way we work with other organisations, and in all our work with children, families and others.

The policy aims to challenge discrimination in all areas of our organisation. We aim to ensure that the Club reflects and meets the needs of the local community and incorporates equal opportunities into all areas of our work.

We aim to make sure that:

- Both the management committee and the staff will try to ensure that the services they provide are accessible to everyone
- This policy will be actively promoted through our decision making, employment practices, play opportunities and service provision, and we will strive to monitor its implementation and its effectiveness in line with changes in legislation and guidance
- All aspects of our Club aim to reflect the diversity found within society

# Healthy eating policy

1. It is our aim to foster and encourage an interest in healthy eating amongst the children by offering a variety of foods from various cultures.
2. All children will be offered a healthy snack on arrival at the Club. This is likely to consist of fresh fruit and vegetables. From time to time, we may offer "treats". We may also offer food from other cultures as part of our activities. Personal diets and parental requests will be followed. Children will be encouraged but not forced to eat. Amounts of food consumed will be moderated in negotiation with individual children. Children will be encouraged to eat at specified times and will have tables available to sit at during these times.
3. All drinks will be either milk or juice based and sugar free. Fresh drinking water will also be readily available to the children at all times during the operation of the Club.
4. Staff preparing food will hold up-to-date food hygiene certificates. Food supplied by the Club will be stored appropriately i.e., refrigerated.
5. Staff will be fully aware of the specific dietary requirements of children and other staff. This information will be taken from that contained within the parent/carer/club contract. Should there be any changes to the information parents/carers give when originally completing this contract then it is their responsibility to inform the play leader of such changes as soon as possible.
6. In order that we can fulfil our commitment to healthy eating, it will be necessary to limit the consumption of sweets or fizzy drinks on the premises. Chewing gum and bubble gum will

be prohibited for health and safety reasons. We, therefore, ask that parents/carers do not provide their children with such items unless there is a specific dietary requirement to do so. In this case, parents/carers should consult with the Senior Playworker in advance.

7.   When sending a packed lunch or tea with your child to the club you should fully consider how it will be stored. We do not have a refrigeration system available to hold individual packed lunches or teas. Parents/carers should therefore not provide packed food that requires storage below room temperature unless they supply an ice pack to accompany the packed lunch or tea.

Examples of items that require an ice pack for safe storage are:
   Dairy products
   Cold cooked meats and poultry
   Fish/shellfish
   We regret we cannot microwave hot snacks for children.
   It is important that parents/carers adhere to this to ensure the welfare and good health of their child. Incorrectly stored food can harbour dangerous bacteria.

## Health care policy

The Club promotes the good health of both children and staff by ensuring the highest standards of premises, equipment maintenance and staff awareness in safety matters.

Staff are informed and aware of the importance of good hygiene practice in order to prevent the spread of infection.

A staff health and safety officer/co-ordinator are responsible for bringing safety issues to the attention of everyone and monitoring all aspects of health and safety.

Staffs responsible for food preparation and handling are fully aware of and comply with regulations relating to food safety and hygiene.

There will always be at least one member of staff holding a current First Aid certificate on the premises or on Club outings.

## Complaints procedure

The Holiday Club aims to provide a high quality, efficient and accessible service to parents and children.

The way that we work is reviewed regularly and we welcome suggestions and constructive criticism to help us maintain a high-quality provision. However, from time to time a parent or child may feel that they have a complaint against some aspect of our club, or an individual member of staff. Usually, it should be possible to resolve any problems as soon as they occur by speaking to the club manager. If not, then you should follow the formal complaints procedure set out below.

## Informal stage

Initially speak to the club manager, if you prefer to do this outside of normal club hours and in confidence, please arrange a convenient time. The manager will make every attempt to resolve the matter and will communicate the outcome to the complainant within 14 days of the complaint being made.

Should you not be satisfied with the outcome then you should move on to the formal complaints procedure.

## Formal – stage 1

1. Put your complaint in writing to the club manager using the club's complaint form. A copy of this form is available from the manager. You should maintain a copy of the completed form along with any other communications on this matter for your own records. The manager will sign and date the form when received and will file it in the club's Complaint Logbook. All communications and actions taken regarding this complaint will be recorded by the manager in the logbook.
2. The manager will acknowledge your complaint in writing as soon as possible and will forward a copy to the club's committee member. The manager will investigate the matter in full consultation with the management committee. Confidentiality will be maintained throughout.
3. Members of staff involved will be asked in a constructive manner to give their account of the matter. No unfounded accusations will be made. If there is any delay in the investigation the manager will advise you of the reasons. You will be kept up to date with what is happening, and you will receive a full reply in writing within 14 days.
4. The response you receive will be copied to the staff members concerned, with recommendations for any action to be taken. A full account of the complaint, the actions taken, and the final outcome will be communicated to the club's management committee. The matter will also be reported at the next management committee meeting. If you are not satisfied with the outcome, you can ask the manager to refer the matter to the next stage.

## Formal – stage 2

1. The manager will refer the complaint and all relevant documentation to the nominated person to act on behalf of the management committee. They will investigate the complaint and how it has been handled by the club manager independently. This may involve convening a special committee meeting.
2. The "responsible individual" will send a response to the complainant within 4 weeks outlining how the complaint was investigated and detailing the final outcome.
3. The decision of the management committee is final.

## Formal – stage 3

1. Should you still be unhappy with this response and feel that if the matter is not resolved to your satisfaction and the club's operation becomes detrimental to the quality of care provided to children and families then you should contact the Care Standards Inspectorate -the body with which this club is registered. Their contact details are as follows:

## Health, safety and hygiene policy

### Health

- The temperature in the rooms will be maintained at not less than 18°C/ 65°F
- There will be no smoking on the premises.
- Children should have some opportunity of access to outdoor play –weather permitting.
- Staff should be aware of any child's special health conditions and appropriate care can then be made available (in consultation with the relevant parent/carer).
- Please do not send your child to the club if he or she is unwell. If your child will not be attending the club due to illness, you must inform the school and club.
- If a child is not feeling well enough to participate, it will be our policy to provide a quiet place to lie down or encourage him/her to participate in a quiet activity. Any child will be observed for any worsening symptoms. Their parents/carer will be notified verbally the same day.
- If a child's condition worsens to such an extent that the play workers are seriously concerned and suspects urgent medical treatment is required, then the parent/carer will be notified immediately and if necessary, an ambulance will be called.
- If a child is exposed to a communicable disease, it will be our policy to contact the parents in writing: likewise, we appreciate parents co-operation if their child comes down with an infectious disease so that the appropriate steps can be taken to notify other club users if necessary.
- The club will keep a register of communicable diseases.
- Medicines will not routinely be administered. If medication is to be given the following practices will be followed

    - **Medicines will not usually be administered unless they have been prescribed for that child by a doctor.**
    - **Medicines will be stored in their original containers clearly labelled with the child's name and not accessible to other children.**
    - **Asthma inhalers will be available to the child at all times.**
    - **Checks will be made to ensure that any medication received into the club is not out of date.**

167

- The parent or guardian will complete the club's medication form before any medication is administered.
- Written records will be kept of all medicines administered to children on the club's approved medication form.
- If the administration of prescription medicines requires technical or medical knowledge, then individual training will be given to staff by the parent/carer and/or a qualified health professional. Training will be specific to the individual child concerned.
- The registered person will confirm that the administration of medication conforms to their insurance cover.

## Safety

- A first aid box will be available, and the contents checked and kept up to date.
- A fire drill notice will be displayed in the rooms.
- Fire drill will be practised once every club and details recorded. This procedure can also be used to evacuate in the event of an emergency. It may be necessary to reverse the above procedure in order to return the children to the building safely and quickly in the event of an emergency outside.
- Equipment will be regularly monitored and checked for safety and the appropriate annual checks will be carried out.
- Equipment will be well maintained.
- All staff will be aware of the correct use of equipment used by the club.
- Children will not have unsupervised access to the Food Preparation room.
- A register of children and adults will be completed at the start of each session.
- Smoke detectors are installed and should be regularly checked, and adequate fire detection and control equipment will be readily available.
- Two adult workers will be present at all times and children will be supervised at **all** times.
- The exits to the building must be kept clear at all times and fire doors should not be obstructed.
- The premises will be checked before locking up at the end of each session.
- A safety check on the premises, both indoor and out will be made at the beginning and end of each session.
- Equipment available will be used according to the manufacturer's instructions.
- An accident book will be available for the reporting of all accidents.
- Potentially hazardous equipment will be securely stored.

## Hygiene

- Children will be encouraged to wash their hands after using the toilet and before eating or cooking. Running water, soap and towels will be available.

- Tissues will be available and disposed of hygienically.
- Staff are aware of how infections, including HIV infections, are transmitted.
- Rubber gloves and disposable aprons will be available for clearing up after spills of bodily fluids.
- Floors and other surfaces will be disinfected when appropriate.
- Spare laundered clothes will be available in case of emergencies.

# Appendix

## 1 Programmes used

### *Boo Zoo*

Boo Zoo was created by Neil Griffiths.

Boo Zoo is a way of learning maths with toy animals and a toy zoo keeper. Students learn maths through playing with the characters and listening to stories about the characters. Boo Zoo contains all the support necessary for staff to plan the activities. More information can be found at https://.redrobinbooks.com and you can watch a YouTube video of it in action at https://youtu.be/C7zvcsHPu4Q

### *Numicon*

Numicon, developed by education publisher OUP, is a resource that is used in many schools to support maths teaching. It is a system of flat plastic shapes with holes in, with each shape representing a number from 1 to 10. Each number has its own colour. It is a concrete representation of numbers 1–10. It has a multi-sensory approach. It is very visual, and children can manipulate and explore them without the risk of breaking them.

More information can be found at https://home.oxfordowl.co.uk and you can watch a YouTube video at https://youtu.be/04o27vMGlk

### *Dough Disco*

Dough Disco™ is a fine muscle exercise that Shonette Bason Wood developed. To find out more and see it in action go to https://youtu.be/9LNOnSM_y_4

# Magic Therapy™

The underlying concepts in magic therapy target areas of motor, psychosocial, cognitive and sensory processing [skills] that lend themselves well to intervention. To see magic therapy in action at our school please go to https://www.bing.com/videos/search?view=detail&mid=6FA3 E31D5DCEF7D4C0FA6FA3E31D5DCEF7D4C0FA&q=magic+therapy+youtube&shtp=GetUrl& shid=cd27a0ce-f257-4994-a599-ca621304bd76&shtk=TWFnaWMgVGhlcmFweSBIRA%3D %3D&shdk=TWFnaWMgVGhlcmFweSBIRA%3D%3D&shhk=%2B6XA0V3nq %2FgbMKiytDW9swrvEiVxtr6qljL5puxXx8I%3D&form=VDSHOT&shth=OSH.1XdF4 ivubFQToKb1QuHfEw

To find out more information go to https://magictherapy.com/

# Tacpac™

Tacpac is an activity that pairs the sensory aspects of sound and touch to promote communication and social interaction as well as sensory, neurological and emotional development. The music used is composed specifically to reflect the texture of each object so that the person receiving Tacpac experiences total sensory alignment. During Tacpac sessions, students are paired one to one with a familiar adult and a playful approach is used. To see a Tacpac session in action at a school please visit https://youtu.be/7x4Tbgu2kcA?list=PL-a5MUplgI4nVMUEFGUGFg4jTxjvPyLur

To find out more visit https://tacpac.co.uk/

# Story Massage™

I read the book Once Upon a Touch in 2016 and was so enthusiastic about its playful approach to telling stories that I discussed it with several staff members and lent them the book. They tried out the stories and wanted to learn the ten simple massage strokes from the authors themselves. I managed to get the founders of Story Massage, Mary, and Sandra, to deliver a training session at one of our International Therapies Conferences that we ran in the October of 2016. They trained some of our staff in the technique and used the video footage as part of their online training for other organisations. To see one of the videos please visit https://youtu.be/89XLtj1Yhjg

Here is a report from a teacher to me in 2019

"Constant usage and staff training has shown an improvement in the results of story massage. This sensory touch activity helps pupils to relax, and some pupils now allow touch. This is proving to be a very important part of the enrichment session. Pupils and staff have worked together to compose their own unique poems and stories, and these are linked to celebrations and activities going on throughout the year. Pupils are proud of their achievements."

For more information on this playful therapy please visit http://www.storymassage.co.uk

## Maker Movement

The maker movement is a social movement with an artisan spirit. Maker culture emphasizes learning-through-doing (active learning) in a social environment. Maker culture emphasizes informal peer-led and shared learning motivated by fun and self-fulfilment. Maker culture has attracted the interest of educators concerned about students' disengagement from traditional teaching. The maker movement was born in America. To find out more go to https://wiki.p2 pfoundation.net/Maker_Movement

# 2 Theories on the Development of Play

## Margaret Parten's Stages of Social Play Theory (1929)

Unoccupied Play – 0–3 months – observes surroundings, displays random movements
Solitary (Independent) Play – 3 months to 2 yrs – Plays alone
Spectator Play – 2 to 2½ yrs – Observes others playing
Parallel Play – 2½ to 3 yrs – Play alongside others not with them
Associate play – 3–4 yrs – Start to interact with others in play. Fleeting cooperation.
Cooperative Play – 4–6+ yrs – Plays together with shared aims.

## Stages of Cognitive Development and Play (Piaget 1936)

Piaget proposed that Play was made up of ages and three stages and is developmental. The cognitive constructivism of Piaget views learners as active constructors of their world view and discoverers of knowledge.

### Stage 1

Sensorimotor-repeated movements such as mouthing objects, lining up objects or banging objects together
    Functional – The use of bodily movements, with or without objects. Running and jumping, sliding, gathering, manipulating objects such as placing objects in a container.
    Constructive – Constructing something such as a tower of blocks, Legos or different materials (sand, modelling clay, paint, blocks) – in an organized way to make something

### Stage 2

Symbolic/Fantasy play is role playing or make-believe play, such as pretending to be a superhero, or monster, and make believe actions, such as using blocks to represent cakes when playing at house.

## Stage 3

Games with rules – Board games, playing tag, etc.

## The Zone of Proximal Development (first written about by Vygotsky 1929)

Vygotsky believed that people can only develop properly through social interaction. He believed that one of the key elements of social development is play. Vygotsky appreciated the role of adults in scaffolding and co-constructing learning with children.

Vygotsky did not break down development into a series of predetermined stages as Piaget did. Vygotsky stressed the important role that culture plays on development. He believed that children play with objects according to the meaning that adults give them and then they learn to symbolically substitute the functions of these objects. He believed they then moved on to socio-dramatic play where children act out the adult world and play the roles of people in that world.

Vygotsky is known for his theory of the Zone of Proximal Development (ZPD)

It was originally developed by Vygotsky to argue against the use of academic, knowledge-based testing. Vygotsky did not complete the work on ZPD, and the definition has been expanded upon since his death. ZPD is an area of learning that occurs when a student is assisted by a teacher, assistant, or peer with a higher skill set. That allows them to expand their possibilities for development.

It is similar in the way that we teach in special schools and we use the traffic light assessment system to track their progress. Red means a task that the student cannot do even with help, Amber means a task that the student can do only with assistance (scaffolding), and Green means a task that the student can now do unaided as a result of that assistance.

Scaffolding happens when the amber light is on and this support is tapered off as the student becomes more able and moves into the green.

## Role Play – Developmental Stages (Shefatya & Smilansky 1990)

1. Imitative role play
2. Make believe using objects
3. Make believe using actions and speech
4. Developing role play for a period of at least 10 minutes
5. Interaction between players
6. Dialogue related play

# 3 The Fifty Four Natural Webstring Self-Evident Senses and Sensitivities

The Radiation Senses

1. Sense of light and sight, including polarized light.
2. Sense of seeing without eyes such as heliotropism or the sun sense of plants.
3. Sense of colour.
4. Sense of moods and identities attached to colours.
5. Sense of awareness of one's own visibility or invisibility and consequent camouflaging.
6. Sensitivity to radiation other than visible light including radio waves, X rays, etc.
7. Sense of Temperature and temperature change.
8. Sense of season including the ability to insulate, hibernate and winter sleep.
9. Electromagnetic sense and polarity which includes the ability to generate current (as in the nervous system and brain waves) or other energies.

The Feeling Senses

10. Hearing including resonance, vibrations, sonar and ultrasonic frequencies.
11. Awareness of pressure, particularly underground, underwater, and to wind and air.
12. Sensitivity to gravity.
13. The sense of excretion for waste elimination and protection from enemies.
14. Feel, particularly touch on the skin.
15. Sense of weight, gravity and balance.
16. Space or proximity sense.
17. Coriolus sense or awareness of effects of the rotation of the Earth.
18. Sense of motion. Body movement sensations and sense of mobility.

The Chemical Senses

19. Smell with and beyond the nose.
20. Taste with and beyond the tongue.
21. Appetite or hunger for food, water and air.
22. Hunting, killing, or food obtaining urges.
23. Humidity sense including thirst, evaporation control and the acumen to find water or evade a flood.
24. Hormonal sense, as to pheromones and other chemical stimuli.

The Mental Senses

25. Pain, external and internal.
26. Mental or spiritual distress.
27. Sense of fear, dread of injury, death, or attack.
    (25–27 are attractions to *seek additional natural attractions* in order to support and strengthen well-being, attractions to run **for** your life. They are part of Nature's attractive dance, not "repulsions")

28. Procreative urges including sex awareness, courting, love, mating, maternity, paternity and raising young.
29. Sense of play, sport, humour, pleasure and laughter.
30. Sense of physical place, navigation senses including detailed awareness of land and seascapes, of the positions of the sun, moon and stars.
31. Sense of time and rhythm.
32. Sense of electromagnetic fields.
33. Sense of weather changes.
34. Sense of emotional place, of community, belonging, support, trust and thankfulness.
35. Sense of self including friendship, companionship and power.
36. Domineering and territorial sense.
37. Colonizing sense including compassion and receptive awareness of one's fellow creatures, sometimes to the degree of being absorbed into a superorganism.
38. Horticultural sense and the ability to cultivate crops, as is done by ants that grow fungus, by fungus who farm algae or birds that leave food to attract their prey.
39. **Language sense,** used to express feelings and convey information in every medium from the bees' dance to *uniquely human* articulation, stories and literature.
40. Sense of humility, appreciation, ethics.
41. Senses of form and design.
42. **Sense of reason,** including memory and the capacity for logic and science.
43. **Sense of mind and consciousness.**
44. Intuition or subconscious deduction.
45. Aesthetic sense, including creativity and appreciation of beauty, music, literature, form, design and drama.
46. Psychic capacity such as foreknowledge, clairvoyance, clairaudience, psychokinesis, astral projection and possibly certain animal instincts and plant sensitivities.
47. Sense of biological and astral time, awareness of past, present and future events.
48. The capacity to hypnotize other creatures.
49. Relaxation and sleep including dreaming, meditation, brain wave awareness.
50. Sense of pupation including cocoon building and metamorphosis.
51. Sense of excessive stress and capitulation.
52. Sense of survival by joining a more established organism.
53. Spiritual sense, including conscience, capacity for sublime love, ecstasy, a sense of sin, profound sorrow and sacrifice.
54. Sense of homeostatic unity, of instinctive *natural attraction* aliveness and survival. The singular essence-diversity attraction dance mother of all our other senses (NNIAAL) and the Big Bang in the now the moment. The love of love, love54.å (See NNIAAL equation and its operation in microorganisms.)

From the work of Guy Murchie, *The Seven Mysteries of Life* and Dr Michael J. Cohen, *Reconnecting to Nature*

# Bibliography

Anderson, A. (2019) *Virtual reality, augmented reality and artificial intelligence in special education.* London and New York: Routledge.

Anderson, A. (2020) *Therapeutic trampolining for children and young people with special educational needs.* London and New York: Routledge.

Anderson, A. (2021) *Music, sound and vibration in special education.* London and New York: Routledge.

Athey, C. (1990, updated 2007) *Extending thought in young children: A parent-teacher partnership.* London: Sage Publications Ltd.

Atkinson, M. & Hooper, S. (2015) *Once upon a touch: Story massage for children.* London and Philadelphia: Singing Dragon.

Axline, V. (1964) *Dibs: In search of self.* New York, NY: Ballantine Books.

Ayres, A. J. (1989) *Sensory integration and praxis tests.* Los Angeles: Western Psychological Services.

Bertram, T. & Pascal, C. (2002) *Early years education: An international perspective.* London: Qualifications and Curriculum Authority.

Bruner, J. S. (1972) *Nature & uses of immaturity.* American Psychologist, 27, 687–708.

Bruner, J. S. (2009) *The process of education.* Cambridge: Harvard University Press.

Bryan, J. (2018) *Eye can write.* London: Lagom Publishers.

Burke, A. & Marsh, J. (Eds.) (2013) *Children's virtual play worlds: Culture, learning and participation.* New York: Peter Lang Publishing.

Burn, A. & Richards C. (Eds.) (2014) *Children's games in the new media age.* London: Routledge.

Buchsbaum, D., Bridgers, S., Skolnick Weisberg, D. & Gopnik, A. (2012) *The power of possibility: Causal learning, counterfactual reasoning, and pretend play.* Philosophical Transactions of the Royal Society B, 367, 2202–2212. doi: 10.1098/rstb.2012.0122.

Cheng, D., Reunamo, J., Cooper, P., Liu, K. & Vong, P. (2015) *Children's agentive orientations in play-based and academically focused preschools in Hong Kong.* Early Child Development and Care, 185, 1–17. doi: 10.1080/03004430.2015.1028400.

Cohen, M. J. (1993) *Counselling with nature: Catalyzing sensory moments that let earth nurture.* Counselling Psychology Quarterly, 6(1), 39–52. doi: 10.1080/09515079308254491

Cohen, M. J. (2007) *Reconnecting with nature.* 3rd edition. Maidstone, Kent: Eco Press.

Corbett, B. A., Gunther, J. R., Comins, D., Price, J., Ryan, N., Simon, D., Schupp, C. W. & Rios, T. (2010) *Brief Report: Theatre as a therapy for children with autism spectrum disorder.* Journal of Autism and Developmental Disorders, 41(4), 505–511. doi: 10.1007/s 10803-010-1064-1. PMID:20640592; PMCID: PMC3055998

Corbett, B. A., Schupp, C. W., Simon, D., Ryan, N. & Mendoza, S. (2010) *Elevated cortisol during play is associated with age and social engagement in children with autism.* Molecular Autism, 1(1), 13. doi: 10.1186/2040-2392-1-13

Corbett, B. A., Swain, D. M., Coke, C., Simon, D., Newsom, C., Houchins-Juarez, N., Jenson, A., Wang, L. & Song, Y. (2014) *Improvement in social deficits in autism spectrum disorders using a theatre-based, peer-mediated intervention.* Autism Research: Official Journal of the International Society for Autism Research, 7(1), 4–16. doi: 10.1002/aur.1341

Couper, L. & Sutherland, D. (2019) *Learning and connecting in school playgrounds.* London and New York: Routledge.

Craig-Unkefer, L. & Kaiser, A. (2003) *Increasing peer-directed social-communication skills of children enrolled in head start.* Journal of Early Intervention, 25, 229–247. doi: 10.1177/105381510302500401.

Csikszentmihalyi, M. (1990) *Flow: The psychology of optimal experience.* New York, NY: Harper and Row.

Dewey, J. (1915a) *Play.* In P. Munroe (Ed.), *A cyclopaedia of education* (Vol. 2, p. 725). New York: The MacMillan Co.

Dewey J (1915b) *Froebel's educational principles chapter 5 in the school and society* (pp. 111–127). Chicago: University of Chicago.

Diamond, A., Barnett, S., Thomas, J. & Munro, S. (2007) *Preschool program improves cognitive control.* Science, 317, 1387. doi: 10.1126/science.1151148

Didehbani, N. (2016) Available online at www.utdallas.edu/news/2016/9/22-32196_VrtualReality-Helps-Children-on-Autism-Spectrum-story-wide.html

Doidge, N. (2008) *The brain that changes Itself: Stories of personal triumph from the frontiers of brain science.* Australia, New Zealand, United Kingdom: Bolinda Publishing Pty Ltd.

Dunn, W. (2007) *Supporting children to participate successfully in everyday life by using sensory processing knowledge.* Journal-Infants and Young Children, 20, 84–101.

Entwistle, H. (1970) *Child-centred education.* London: Methuen.

Ginsburg, K. R., Milteer, R. M. & Wood, D. L. (2011) *The importance in play in promoting healthy child development and maintaining strong parent-child bond: Focus on children in poverty.* Newsletter American Academy of Paediatrics, 129(1), e204–e214.

Goffman, E. (1955) *On face work: An analysis of ritual elements in social interaction.* Interpersonal and Biological Processes, 18(3), 213–231.

Goffman, E. (1974) *Frame analysis: An essay on the organisation of experience.* Cambridge, Massachusetts: Harvard University Press.

Gray, P. (2013) *Free to learn: Why unleashing the instinct to play will make our children Happier, more self-reliant, and better students for life.* New York: Basic Books.

Greenspan, S. I. & Weider, S. (1997) *Developmental patterns and outcomes in infants and children with disorders in relating and communication: A chart review of 200 cases of children with autistic spectrum disorders.* Journal of Developmental and Learning Disorders, 1(1), 87–141.

Greenspan, S. I. & Weider, S. (1998) *The child with special needs: Encouraging intellectual and emotional growth.* Reading,Massachusetts: Perseus Books.

Gussin Paley, V. (1991) *The boy who would be a helicopter: Uses of storytelling in the classroom.* London, England: Harvard University Press.

Gussin Paley, V. (1993) *You can't say you can't play.* Cambridge, Massachusetts and London, England: Harvard University Press.

Hendy, L. & Toon, L. (2001) *Supporting drama and imaginative play in the early years.* Charlottesville, VA: University of Virginia Press.

Holt, J. (2017) *How children learn, 50th anniversary edition.* New York: Hachette Audio.

Howard, J. & McInnes, K. (2013) *The impact of children's perception of an activity as play rather than not play on emotional well-being.* Child Care, Health and Development, 39(5), 737–742.

Hughes, B. (2002) *A playworkers taxonomy of play types*. 2nd edition. London: Playlink.

Ihlen H. (2018) *Nederlandse nereniging drama therapy*. Netherlands: OaDt.

Josman, N. & Weis, T. (2008) Haifa research team: *Effectiveness of virtual reality for teaching street crossing skills to children and adolescents with autism*. Israel: Haifa University. Available online at http://bit.ly/sc235-33

LeGoff, D.B. (2004) *Use of LEGO as a therapeutic medium for improving social competence* J Autism Dev Disord, 34(5), 557–571. doi: 10.1007/s10803-004-2550-0, PMID: 15628609.

Liffer, K. (2011) *Overview of play: Its uses and importance in early intervention/Early childhood special education*. Infants and Young Children, 24(3), 225–245. doi: 10.1097/IYC.0b013e31821e995c

Lillard, A., Lerner, M., Hopkins, E., Dore, R., Smith, E. & Palmquist, C. (2013) *The impact of pretend play on children's development: A review of the evidence*. Psychological Bulletin, 139(1), 1–34. doi:10.1037/a0029321.

Lloyd George, D. (1926).

Minsky, M. (1975) *Minsky's frame system theory*. Proceedings of the 1975 workshop on theoretical issues in natural language processing (acm.org). Tinlap.

Montessori, M. (1967) *The absorbent mind*. New York, NY: Holt, Rinehart & Winston.

Moreno, Z. T., Blomkvist, L. D. & Rutzel, T. (2000) *Psychodrama, surplus reality, and the art of healing*. Hove, East Sussex: Routledge.

Muentener, P., Herrig, E., & Schulz, L. (2018) *The efficiency of infants' exploratory play is related to longer-term cognitive development*. Frontiers in Psychology, 9, 635. doi: 10.3389/fpsyg.2018.00635.

NAEYC (National Association for the Education of Young Children). (2009) *Developmentally appropriate practice in early childhood programs serving children from birth through Age 8*. National Association for the Education of Young Children position statement, Available at http://www.naeyc.org/files/naeyc/file/positions/PSDAP.pdf

Okimoto, A. M., Bundy, A. & Hanzlik, J. (2000) Playfulness *in children with and without disability: Measurement and intervention*. American Occupational Therapy Association, 54(1), 73–82. doi: 10.5014.1.73. PMID:10686630

Parten, M. B. (1932) *Social participation among pre-school children*. The Journal of Abnormal and Social Psychology, 27(3), 243–269. doi: https://doi.org/10.1037/h0074524

Pellegrini, A. & Bjorklund, D. (1997) *The role of recess in children's cognitive performance*. Educational Psychologist, 32, 35–40. doi: 10.1207/s15326985ep3201_3.

Piaget, J. (1962) *Play, dreams, and imitation in childhood*. New York, NY: Norton.

Play Scotland (November 2020) *Guidelines for unregulated informal play services*. Available online from http://www.playscotland.org

Pizzo, L. & Bruce, S. M. (2010) *Language and play in students with multiple disabilities and visual impairments or deaf-blindness*. Journal of Visual Impairment & Blindness, 104(5), 287–297.

Quinn, J. M. & Rubin, K. H. (1984) *The play of handicapped children*. In T. D. Yawkey & A. D. Pellegrini (Eds.), *Child's play: Developmental and applied* (pp. 63-80). Hillsdale, NJ: Lawrence Erlbaum.

Rios-Rincon, A. M., Adams, K., Magill-Evans, J. & Cook, A. (2016) *Playfulness in children with limited motor abilities when using a Robot*. Physical & Occupational Therapy in Pediatrics, 36(3), 232–246. doi: 10.3109/01942638.2015. 1076559.Epub2015 Nov 13. PMID: 26566226.

Robinson, P. (2016) "Remembering Pokémon Go, the Craze that Swept July 2016". Vice LLC. Available online at www.vice.com/en_uk/article/xdmpgq/remembering-pokemon-go-the-craze-that-swept-july-2016

Roley, S., Mailloux, Z., Miller-Kuhaneck, H. & Glennon, T. (2007) *Understanding ayres sensory integration*. OT Practice, 12(17), CE1–CE8.

Rubin, K., Fein, G. & Vandenberg, B. (1983) *Play*. In E. M. Hetherington (Ed.), *Handbook of child psychology: Socialization, personality, social development: Socialization, personality, social development* (Vol. 4, pp. 694–759). New York, NY: Wiley.

Sahlberg, P. & Doyle, W. (2019) *Let the children play*. UK: Oxford University Press.

Shakespeare, W. (1623) *As you like it*. UK: First Folio.

Smith, Peter K. & Dutton, Susan (1979) *Play and training in direct and innovative problem solving*. Child Development, 50(3), 830–836.

Stenros, J. (2014) *In defence of a magic circle: The social, mental and cultural boundaries of play*. Todigra.org, 1(2). ISSN2328-9422

Stephen, C., Dunlop, A. W. & Trevarthen, C. (2003) *Meeting the needs of children from birth to three: Research evidence and implications for out-of-Home provision*. Scottish Executive Education Department.

Tait, P. (1972) *Behavior of young blind children in a controlled play session*. Perception and Motor Skills, 31, 963–969.

Trawick-Smith, J. (2020) *Young children's play, development, disabilities, and diversity*. New York and London: Routledge.

Tröster, H. & Bambring, M. (1994) *The play behavior and play materials of blind and sighted infants and preschoolers*. Journal of Visual Impairment and Blindness, 88, 421–432.

Tulving, E. (1985) *Elements of episodic memory* (Oxford Psychology Series). USA: Oxford University Press.

United Nations (1989) *What is the convention on the rights of the child?* UNICEF.

Vygotsky, L. S. (1929) *The problem of the cultural development of the child 11*. Journal of Genetic Psychology, 36, 415–432.

Vygotsky, L. S. (1978) *Mind in society: The development of higher psychological processes*. Cambridge, MA: Harvard University Press.

Weisberg, D., Hirsh-Pasek, K. & Golinkoff, R. (2013) *Guided play: Where curricular goals meet a playful pedagogy*. Mind, Brain, and Education, 7, 104–112. doi: 10.1111/mbe.12015.

WAG Welsh Assembly Government (2010) Available online at 100426curriculumforlearnersenORIG.pdf (ioe.ac.uk).

Welsh Government (February 2021) *Guidance for parents and childcare under alert level 4. available online from https://gov.wales/childcare-and-play-alert-level-4-frequentl-asked-questions

Whitebread, D., Neale, D., Jensen, H., Liu, C., Solis, S. L., Hopkins, E., Hirsh-Pasek, K. & Zosh, J. M. (2017) *The role of play in children's development: A review of the evidence (research summary)*. Denmark: The LEGO Foundation, DK.

# Index